Teachers' Secrets
and
Motherhood Savvy
for Homeschoolers

**Grab these ideas and you'll gain
confidence and capability in the place
where it matters most—the home.**

RENÉE ELLISON

Strategies for parenting, child training, homeschooling, and home management by veteran teacher and homeschooler Renée Ellison

~~~~~~

Published by Cross-Over, DBA Homeschool How-To's
Website: http://www.homeschoolhowtos.com
Email: info@homeschoolhowtos.com
Printed in the United States of America

Library of Congress Cataloging-in-Publication Data

Ellison, Renée.
Teachers' secrets and motherhood savvy for homeschoolers/ Renée Ellison.
Durango, Colo.: Homeschool How-To's, c2011.   Updated and revised 2015.
236 p.; 22 cm.
The power of a focused mother—How to train your children, not just discipline them—12 optimal ways to trigger the brain with any subject matter—Turn-your-head home management strategies.
Motherhood—Religious aspects—Christianity.
Mothers—Life skills guides.
Parenting—Religious aspects—Christianity.
Family—Biblical teaching.
Parent and child—Biblical teaching.
Child rearing—Religious aspects—Christianity.
Discipline of children—Biblical teaching.
Home schooling.
Education—Parent participation.
Home economics.
HQ759.46 E55   2011
649.64

ISBN: 0974945587
ISBN-13: 9780974945583

Cover design by Erin Jones. Brain triggers illustrated by Theanna Sparrow.

CONTENTS

For 100's of how-to helps, blogs and podcasts
by Renée Ellison, visit

http://homeschoolhowtos.com/

Part 1:

The Power of a Focused Mother

A lanky teenage boy sauntered up to his mother one summer afternoon and said, "Hey mom, will you come outside and play basketball with me?" "Well, son, I'd love to do that, and I'm honored that you asked me,  but you know I couldn't jump if my life depended on it. How do you imagine I could play basketball with you, dear?" "Oh come on, Mom. It'll be easy. I'll make all the baskets and you just say wonderful!"

There you have it in a nutshell—the essence of motherhood. Most of mothering is all about this sort of nurture and affirmation. Sadly, there is not much of that happening today. Fewer and fewer homes have it. When we look for a culprit, could part of the problem be that, in this generation, we have a whole battalion of preoccupied mothers?

There is much to distract a mother nowadays. But while she is unendingly preoccupied, her children are silently losing important pieces of their childhood. Many mothers are not even aware that this is happening. These losses are deep and irretrievable. Let's take a good look at this trend and where it leads. And then let's look at how and where to raise our focus and sharpen our aim, so that our children grow up spiritually and emotionally strong, the way God intended. The impact of a focused mother is huge and blessed. You can spot the difference in her children a mile off.

The present state

The report card on the past generation is frightening. It shows a record-breaking rate of failure at keeping marriages together. The number of financial bankruptcies is the highest in recorded history. This generation has some of the lowest test scores among the industrialized nations, and throngs are living dissipated lives filled with mindless entertainment. Employers hire from an ever-decreasing pool of people who actually know how to work (or even *desire* to), much less know how to fill out applications. There are more people on anti-depressant drugs than at any other period of history. High school counselors' offices are jammed with more students than they can handle. Childhood obesity and diabetes are epidemic. And in some regions it seems that the casinos that now dot our land will soon outnumber our churches. This generation is full of individuals, each of whom was some mother's child.

Without realizing it, many mothers have become trapped in externals—how they look and how their house looks. They live in catalogs and stores and athletic centers covered with large mirrors. Others live for happenings, movies, comings and goings, entertainments. Some live for others outside the home—friends and extended family. Retrogressively, they find themselves overly absorbed with their own birth family, rather than focusing on their immediate family-in-the-making. Others are absorbed in making money, be it little amounts or big, personal projects, and/or hobbies. Meanwhile, the days march inexorably onward. Children grow up, day in and day out, without a mother's loving, focused attentiveness.

It should be a child's birthright to have a mother inside the back door screen when he bounds in from play for supper. But this birthright has been stolen from the majority of children in our nation today. Over the past three decades, a missing vision of what motherhood really *is* has brought ruin to our culture. We're dying from within, just like Rome did.

Dashed expectations

How did this happen? If the enemy can't physically remove a mother from her children by death, disease, abandonment, day care, or a full-time job outside the home, he moves to Plan B. He artfully distracts her and preoccupies her day after day until childhood is over. The net effect is the same. And this is where we find many mothers and their children today: robbed, but they don't know it yet.

A child has an expectation that his mother will, at the very least, notice him and, much more than that, have a steady, caring way with him. If his expectations are routinely dashed, there comes a day when something breaks in his little heart. He learns to not lift his head to look anymore.

He makes a mental note that his mother is always on the other end of... her smart phone, her iPad, her laptop, her seminar, her advanced coursework, her hobby, her neighborhood get-together, her part-time job, her church group, her shopping, her car, her errands, her house, her mother, her friends. The unmistakable daily message to the child becomes "Everyone else is always more important." And something dies.

Little children instinctively look to their mothers. Their little chatter about their pet frog, today, becomes the crucial conversation about who they will marry, tomorrow. If you didn't care about the frog, one day they won't bother you with any discussion about their future mate.

If you were to tabulate the actual minutes that you spent focused upon each of your children today, face to face and side by side, how many minutes would it have been? How many minutes was it yesterday? Where is your child, really, on your list of priorities?

The bottom line is that children suffer because of mothers who are missing in action. The throngs of moms who are preoccupied with these dazzling dead-end activities and over-relating with adult friends (who were once OTHER people's small children) are doing so in preference of their own children.

Your willingness to nurture your own children is more significant than you know. It is a spiritual secret how big the impact will be for all eternity. YOU can't know now—not until the day when the Heavenly Father rewards His people for the works they have done (Revelation 22:12). Simply believe it, because God tells you in His Word to do it. Begin to beam more and more love upon your children.

~~~~~~~~~~~~

To recover right perspectives about all of this, let's find out who YOU are, first.

Upping your role

Focused motherhood begins with having a high view of your own God-given worth and of the high role God gave you in your family. Most mothers have very little idea of what they mean to their children. Therefore, they don't treasure developing their role very much. They don't pour very much into it because they don't see into the future very well. They view motherhood casually, as a necessity, as mere maintenance, rather than something to lay hold of eagerly. Conversely, one mother had the *right* idea when she was asked if she'd prefer not to be a stay-at-home mom. "Are you kidding?! I don't want *money*, I want *power*!" Such a woman is rare these days.

Work to diminish your distractions, and seek to build up your grand estate of motherhood, in hopes of becoming a tower of stability for your children's emerging lives. Manicure your broad and vast psychological family grounds so you send forth secure children into the world. Rearrange your emotional furniture optimally for what's ahead in your children's lives, not your own. Refine your motherhood, polish it, improve it, prize every day of it, and expect great results.

To regain perspective about how important motherhood is, let's begin by looking at what you mean to your child before you even get out of bed in the morning. What is a mother, to a child? If mothers knew the full impact of who God designed them to be, they would, no doubt, tremble. Check this out: even if you are a rotten mother, a drug addict who abandoned your child as a baby, your child will still spend the rest of his life looking for you.

Many orphans have a strong desire to find their birth mother (even though they retain a deep love for their adoptive mother). When huge, triumphant football players are interviewed on national TV, who do they wave to? Their *mothers*!

Jailed criminals, too, are known to think fondly of their mothers in between crimes. Politicians boast, "It was my mother who made me great." Preachers refer to the spiritual roots they gained at their mother's knee.

Just the fact that you EXIST is a stabilizing force in a child's developing psyche. When people hear that their mother has just died, even when they themselves are adults, there is often a "deer-in-the-headlights" realization that no one will ever again care if they fall and scrape their knee or not! Not *really* care.

This is the bottom line: the awesome realization about motherhood is that, if you want to have a profound influence on your children, you don't have to *do* anything but *be there*. So if you are having an awful day, have no energy, and find yourself on the couch, cheer up and remember that just your presence is an anchor in your child's life.

You have value to your child—every time you pass through a room, or even every time he merely hears your voice in the next room. You have value to your child, even if he travels overseas and can't speak to you for several years. Your existence *somewhere on the planet* makes his days go better.

The absence of a mother starts a child out with an emotional handicap. So, purpose to believe and act upon the fact that you are an irreplaceable reference point for others in your family. *With* you, they become one thing; *without* you, some part of them always quakes. Therefore, determine to *be* their mother. Don't be always somewhere else in your thought-life or activities. *Be* there.

What to do

All the discussion up to this point has been about the value of just your existence. You haven't *done* anything yet! Now if you actually *look* at your child, smile at him, talk with him, take interest in him, your influence goes through the roof. Then, if you ratchet up your efforts just one last notch by *purposing* to educate him, to train him, discipline, encourage, and refine him, your influence goes into the stratosphere.

So, to shift gears to be this kind of mother, you must begin with the end in view. All meaningful effort begins with a well-defined strong vision of specifically where you are actually headed. Instead of viewing rearing children as an inconvenience to what you'd rather be doing, you begin to view rearing a family as an investment.

Your investment

Having a child is an investment. A parent can either pour a great deal into them or barely invest in them at all. Like a farmer, your expectations for the size and kind of yield you want determine how much you are willing to plant and how hard you're willing to work at it, every day. You make this decision *way up front.* If you only plant 10 seeds and then go read magazines and eat bonbons for the rest of the summer, you are not preparing to win some 4-H contest with your garden. On the other hand, if you plant several acres, roll up your sleeves, and get out there to work your land every morning at daybreak and say no to daily baseball games every afternoon, you expect your land to yield a great harvest. Where your focus is, there will be your reward.

Invest big in your children, and some day your buttons will pop right off your shirt with pride. Invest little—every time you think something *else* is more important—and you'll be ashamed at what they become. If you want thoroughbreds, you have to train thoroughbreds! You've gotta feed 'em like thoroughbreds, groom and dress 'em like thoroughbreds, work 'em like thoroughbreds, school 'em like thoroughbreds, control and discipline their time like thoroughbreds, and enter them in real life skirmishes/demands incrementally and progressively until they become full blown, capable champions. That is what royalty does. From the nursery to the coronation day, they train their offspring to be the best that they can possibly be. That is why they tutor them and don't send them to public schools—so they don't lose a day of surveillance on the progress of their dynasty. They focus, focus, focus on the end results.

What many mothers fail to realize is that they have an opportunity handed to them, during their children's childhoods, to fashion their own future best friends. If you invest a great deal in your children you will want them for your best friends. You will be bursting with pride to be connected to them. But conversely, if you ignore and neglect your children when they are young, their hearts will grow far from you. They will embarrass you; you won't like them as adults; you won't want to be associated with them or be around them. You'll feel shame and failure.

Step back and visualize yourself creating a dynasty, the centerfold picture of Who's Who in Influential Families. You are raising royal children who will shape and rule the culture. Determine to have a strongly bonded and loyal family, a skilled and accomplished family, a family that raises the neighbors' eyebrows in awe and brings glory to God. This sort of family is fueled by the fires of personal sacrifice on the altar of motherhood—choosing your children over yourself, hour by hour, day after day. Fathers are vital to this entire process. If you're fuzzy on that point, just examine the results of the fatherless ghettos in America. This, however, is a book about sparking motherhood.

In the 1800s, the impact of two very different families was traced through several generations. One was the household of two drunkards who cost the state hundreds of thousands of dollars in destruction, crime, rehabilitation, and jailings through three generations. The other was the family of Jonathan and Sarah Edwards whose ensuing generations gave the U.S. three of its early vice presidents, many influential lawyers, preachers, sterling hard-working successful businessmen, and presidents of several colleges, raising both the academic and economic level of the entire nation. Sarah chose to invest in her family. Throughout their 31 years of marriage she considered it her spiritual duty to keep her focus on the home she was creating and managing. She nurtured their 11 children in a peaceful, cheerful, productive, structured blessed home that, even at that time, stood out as noteworthy to English evangelist George Whitefield and others who visited them.

Having said all this, we must guard ourselves against the other extreme of thinking the family is our own personal possession, the source of our own glory. Satisfaction, yes, but with a full awareness that it belongs to our Creator who both birthed it and sustained it. Ours is a job of stewardship only. Stewards have an openhanded joy of being near it all as it happens, but they are content to pass the glory on to the owner.

The key to successful mothering: Focusing and nurturing

Here's the underlying principle: whatever it is that we focus upon and tend to will *prosper*; what we neglect will *falter*. The power of a strong well-identified focus always leads to vaulting advantage and advancement for all involved. So, where we focus is crucial.

Case in point: we have two trees in our front yard that we planted years ago. We grew them from mere twigs that we rooted in a bucket. Finally, we planted them—both on the same day, in the same soil in our front yard. Today, one of those trees towers over our home at a full 25 feet; the other is only four feet tall. The only difference was water. We watered one; the other one was slightly out of reach of the hose, too much trouble to water consistently, so we gave it a hit-or-miss watering. The difference in the results in only a few years is staggering. Let's say it again: what we deliberately focus upon, and carefully tend to, will flourish; what we ignore will disappoint us.

Perhaps this is the reason God begins our career of raising children with nursing!!! God is not a poor investor. Not only does He get your child fed this way, but every time your child has to nurse, you're forced to stop and look at him. It is as if God put a big flashing neon sign on your chest, for your child to see, that says "Dairy Queen—Focus here!" And at the same time, He brings your child up close and personal: she's in your face (i.e., on your chest). And from *your* perspective, your nursing child becomes a lip-smacking, cooing, chortling, surround-sound billboard that gets your attention. God designed it all, as if to say, "Focus here, mom! Ain't I a beaut!"

So, too, as the child grows, academics and chores are a "Focus HERE" means to the same end: relationship! This is the real theater in which the everyday drama of life gets played out. Daily you are choosing whether you want to be onstage with your children, or lost in the audience somewhere, distracted, forever talking to a friend.

The upshot of all this is that the focused mother will aim to mature her children in three areas: their emotions, their self-discipline, and their academic development.

Focused emotional training

Absorbed mothers often miss the enormity of their children's emotional needs. To get a feel for how big their emotional world is, think of your own. Think of all of your own emotional needs today. Didn't the understanding ear of your husband, or some private prayer time, help you gain your equilibrium, charge you up to go again, center you, and establish you? Your child is a tiny adult who has the same large world of real need related to him. He just can't articulate it as well, and doesn't know how to help himself. He'll either get those needs and emotional understanding met in you, or learn to meet those needs somewhere else via daydreaming, in self-defeating behavior, or in some other less desirable relationship.

A large part of training your child to mature in his emotions is to help interpret what happens to him in light of spiritual verities. For example: discouragement can be described as a wounded self-love. The more we renounce self and live for God, the less we have to be disappointed about. Suffering always gains us a depth of maturity. The mother can put a powerful positive spin on even the toughest of childhood emotions.

Focused discipline training

Not only are we not noticing our children, we aren't training them, either. Raising a child can be likened to inheriting a pet baby elephant that plays in your kitchen. The time for shaping his character is woefully short. If, right now, at this very hour, you do not lead him outside, teach him to eat from a trough, and wrap his trunk around logs, learning to haul wood in order to do something meaningful with his life, what is cute today will grow to take over your whole kitchen tomorrow. In just a few short years your elephant will wedge himself between your kitchen walls and stand there stubbornly forever. If he feels ornery enough, he will soon be putting his trunk in your kitchen sink and gleefully spraying water in your face! And when he feels like sitting down, he'll settle himself upon your entire kitchen table and you'll just have to wait until he decides to move. He'll use up all the oxygen in that small room and you'll be reduced to the floor. Eventually you'll find yourself crawling through his legs to escape, running pell-mell out the front door.

Therefore, run ahead of your children in creating opportunities to train them. If you'll do this you'll minimize the need to discipline them so much. Instead of putting out fires all day by having to discipline your children every time you turn around, the new structure, routine, and attention will calm them down. See to it that each child gets the opportunity to reach his full potential in every area of his life, and his needs for discipline will begin to melt away. Your child can't be turning into an Olympic gold medalist and a bum at the same time.

Childhood is a 100-yard dash across time. The frolicking, frisking, carefree stage is painfully short. Their eyes are open and their hearts are open to you today, but for only one short chapter. There comes a day, far sooner than you imagine, when the door of influence slams shut, and emerging adulthood takes over. If you haven't thoroughly and solidly imbued your child with your values before, you can only hope for a minimal influence later. If, at the end of that chapter, the child hasn't internalized your influence, making it his own, he'll cast it off in favor of his own judgment. Because that is what adulthood is all about: actualizing oneself, who one is going to be, via one's own judgment. The time of influence is now. Every day counts. People in other centuries took this job seriously.

Madame Guyon (1648 -1717) wrote the following about training her own daughter: "I had endeavored with Divine assistance to eradicate her faults, and to dispose her to have no will of her own, which is the best disposition for a child."

Guyon's maid remarked on what Guyon taught her about self-discipline: "She taught me the great lesson of self-denial. I never can forget the diligence she used, the patience she exhibited, and the holy love which animated her on my behalf."

Francois Fenelon, Archbishop of Cambry in France in the late 17th- early 18th centuries, wrote to a distinguished woman of the era on discipline: "This, Madame, is your work: to make the service of Jesus Christ prominent in your household, to bring up your family solely for Him, to train it in indifference to the world, in gentleness, patience, modesty, and a real love of God. Examine whether you are doing this, and HOW you are doing it."

Focused academics and chores

Millions of families have discovered that homeschooling provides optimal opportunities for serious ongoing nurturing. Having to do academics and chores around the home can really be an excuse for developing wonderful relationships with your children! Doing these two activities over and over is the setting in which it all happens.

Could it be that our Maker designed a young child's life this way, on purpose when He required parents to train their children? (Deuteronomy chapters 4 through 6)

A focused mother can see to it that she varies her children's circumstances, increasingly exposing them to new materials, events, discussions, people, opportunities and life skills. Your goal is to groom a thoroughly capable adult. While they are yet under your wing, see to it that they are well-rounded, aware, well-versed, and familiar with as much as life can throw at them as possible. Increasing their mental and spiritual stimulation is the name of the game. Get your children on course, and be their main cheerleader all the way through life!

Practically speaking, the optimal way to focus your motherhood on your children is progressive line-upon-line structure in the morning and enlarging experiences in the afternoon. Those enlarging activities could include short half-day mentoring situations, aerobics and weight training, musical development, and home based businesses, for starters!

Navigational tools

The following three tools are vital first steps to increasing your focus upon your children:

Navigational tool #1: **Stop spreading yourself too thin.** Say no. The superwoman myth that had a grip on all of us for the past two decades is *over*. Radical feminism told us that we could have both a job and a home. We, however, lost the prize of the home. When we had to juggle balls to fit it all in, it was always the home ball that we dropped. Instead of a double blessing, we inherited a double curse. Now the career woman carries the curse of the man's world, in addition to her load at home. Every activity occupies space and time, and two activities cannot occupy the same space. Something will remain undone—usually some necessary home chores that don't go away. When we come home to it, there it is, still staring us in the face—in addition to the loss of many nurturing moments that didn't happen with our children *again*, today.

This is not to imply that mothers of young children are never to do anything extra, or are never to talk with friends anymore. We all need that occasionally, but we should be alert to the proportion of time we give to those activities. Is it out of proportion to the huge gaping needs of a growing family that only we can supply?

Navigational tool #2: **Wake up to a day defined by academics and** WORK. Consider cutting down the time that you live for pleasure, for the next movie, the next meal out, the next novel event, or hours on the phone or computer. Concentrate on doing chores and academics together, alternating first one and then the other until the day's allotted work is completely conquered. Teach your children thorough, polished work habits. "Is the stove wiped off, too?" "Did you correct your work and sign and date it and return your books to the exact spot?"

Fix dinner first thing in the morning. Stay focused on completing these priorities, first. Do what you ought to do instead of what you want to do. By your own example, teach your children the principle of "work before pleasure," and eventually their work will become their pleasure. They will cultivate a growing satisfaction with becoming productive. This godly emphasis, day after day, will grow emotionally mature children. If, by your own example, you teach them to work with cheerful, "can-do" attitudes, you give them the gift of self-control and self-mastery for life. It is vital that you work right next to them, and with them, as much as possible. Most attitudes are caught, not taught.

Navigational tool #3: **Use pencil-power to sharpen your focus.** Before you start (preferably the night before), write down a prioritized list of what specifically it is that you plan to accomplish in a day. In addition, have a rou- tine daily check-off progress chart for both academics and chores up on the wall for each child (at a height each child can reach, in a high traffic area), and see to it that they use them. That way you can keep track of where all your children are, in their day's activities, at a glance. Don't worry about putting time-slots on these things, or stressing about starting precisely at 7 or 8 or 9 a.m. They can do each of these activities for just 15 minutes each. The important thing is that your children get through them all each day, not *when* they did them.

Before you embark on any hobby or on any other personally pleasurable activity, get in the discipline of writing down your week's menus. (A side effect of this will be that you'll have the ingredients well-stocked because you wrote them down and bought them, already.) If you'll write down your menu plans, the meals will practically cook themselves! The effort is *all* in the thought. Conquer this habit, and you'll melt that fortress of "kitchen fear!" Preparation replaces panic.

Cheerfulness: The golden attitude of nurture

In and through it all, regardless of what shape you're in, smile at your children—a warm, endearing smile. Smile in the middle of jobs, tasks, and undertakings. Smile at your shy child; smile frequently at your noisy child; smile even more at your most difficult child. This is important work. For what reason? Because each of your children know, deep down in their soul, that if they aren't the apple of their mother's eye, they can't hope to mean much to anyone else.

Cultivate a caring attitude and a cheerful spirit around your children. Even if you don't feel like it, put cheerfulness on like a robe. Think of what you can give of yourself to your children today, not what you aren't getting from your husband. This shift of focus will give you hope and a new release of energy. It is every mother's challenge. We were created to give to our children emotional security through thick and through thin.

Nurture, nurture, nurture. Give affirmation, and beam high-voltage love on all around you. If you'll do this, you'll soon discover that you have a never ending supply because our heavenly Father replenishes it as fast as you give it out.

We may THINK that we, as mothers, are emotionally bankrupt today and need lots of encouragement and time with other adults, but we, in many cases, are not nearly as bankrupt as our children. We must constantly ask ourselves, "Would I want *me* for a mother?"

Let us gladly marshal our wandering affections to think frequently about the power of a focused mother and purpose to be one. The words, "Well done, good and faithful mother" spoken over us, at the end of the ages, will be reward, indeed.

Having said all that, you are now probably teetering precariously somewhere between inspiration and despair. At first you didn't have the vision, but now that you see the light, you feel utterly overwhelmed. You're thinking things like, "I could never do all that! I'm a total failure! It's impossible!"

How do you start?

As we've already mentioned, saying no to everything else is your starting place. But even after you say "NO," there is a battle with yourself ahead. Saddle in for a difficult transition. Once you've determined to come home, emotionally, and are finally staring at what that means, you're apt to feel low—really low. But, cheer up! By finally facing reality, you're actually ahead. You have to come face to face with what has become a dismal pattern, in order for you to *want* conversion. No preparation and no nice dinner on the table night after night; children constantly bickering; not much schooling happening; constant stress and panic—these can someday turn around into a smoothly running happy home. And it starts by saying "No" to other things.

Your next stage is to form the habit of steadily thinking about the end results—raising godly mature capable children. Someone stepped up to Thomas Edison one day and said, "How did you ever come up with such a marvelous invention?" He replied, "Through always thinking about it!" Steady focused thought will get you there. Everything we do begins in the mind, whether we're conscious of it or not. Every successful business was started in someone's mind; every university began with a single thought in that direction. Picture yourself as one of those storybook mothers. Aim to be an utterly capable, confident, charming housewife and mother! It begins with a true picture of what God intends. For a while, go to bed with Titus 2:5, and get up with Proverbs 31:27.

One-a-day's

Each day, make yourself do something to maintain/spiff up your home—a task you'd rather not do, even one that you *dread* doing. Set the timer for 15 minutes, go do it, and then quit when the bell rings. Tomorrow, do the same. Ready, set, go. Do one thing that you can't stand to do, and do it first thing in the morning. Immediately after devotions, conquer making dinner. This guarantees joy later in the day.

Now, let me share a personal example of the way one works out of domestic sloth into skill. Because I was a career woman first and got married later in life (at age 38), I was not acquainted with a kitchen. I could easily grade 125 themes a night and plan my English lecture for the morrow, but cooking dinner was sheer terror. After the wedding, I took myself in hand.

I applied the formula. First, I said "no" to everything else. However, much to my surprise, I could find a million things to do *at home* that still kept me from entering the kitchen. So next, for a while I had to make it my top priority to make our dinner. And I mean TOP priority—higher even than taking a shower!—because I was so out of hand in this area. I carried on internal conversations like, "No, you are not going to water the plants now." "No, you are not going to mend the button." "No, you are not going to exercise yet," etc. Still it was no good. I would sit and stare at the kitchen. Because my body was not in the habit of bustling about, but rather sitting grading papers, I even had to retrain my autonomic nervous system. It seemed I would never cross that Jordan. It seemed Herculean. I was out of my comfort zone; my natural abilities were no help at all. So I sat and stared some more. I begged God to help me. Where do I start?

In a quiet little voice, He taught me a spiritual principle: just move in that direction. Do some little thing. Do some tiny effort toward that goal. Offer Him your little loaves and fishes of clumsy action. So I said, okay, I can clean a kitchen cupboard (though that still kept me from cooking dinner)! Nevertheless, that one small effort broke the ice. Soon I was cleaning many cupboards, then I was making lists of tools needed and food needed, and finally I cooked some simple, unskilled, inglorious thing for dinner. But two things happened: I began a habit (dinner was actually made in the morning), and I had made an inroad to mastering my kitchen and me.

I had a similar struggle over planning menus and writing them down. I couldn't imagine anything worse. It felt like planning a trip to the Arctic. I'd never been there, and I didn't know what to take. I stared at that blank paper for a long time, and again the distractions presented them- selves: "Go help the neighbor...go get the mail...just go anywhere but here!" I hog-tied and sat on myself. I started by just placing my pencil down on that paper. I told myself, just make little boxes, and then add the days of the week. Hey, that was sort of fun! Then I reasoned that it was best to look in the cupboards to see what I al- ready had that I could cook with ...'twould be cheaper that way. So I looked in all the cupboards, and meticulously proceeded through every shelf, pushing cans aside and looking into the dark recesses of the cupboard (again, an escape from actually having to cook the thing) and wrote down something that could be made into a meal, if I added a little somethin' with it. My next "outing" was to see what I had stored in the fridge and then it was on to take a look at my freezer storage. By just taking those three "field trips," my menus were planned for a week. (For more on this, order our how-to #22: *What? I Have to Fix Dinner Again?!*) It took me all morning, but it was a start. Soon I would do in minutes, in all sorts of household skills, what took me forever, in the beginning.

Even when we imagine that we are on the right track by flipping through a recipe book (at least it's not time wasted on a magazine), however, we can lose our way looking and looking and still not get dinner on the table. So, the next thing I learned was to plan just one week of meals and then repeat that week's meals over and over until it was a conquered, mindless skill. The goal was to be able to fix dinner *while* talking to family or houseguests. Over time, I applied this pattern to area after area in my home.

Now if another weak area for you is homeschooling, if you find that you can't stand it either, don't know how to do it, and can't face it, apply the same principle. Just begin. Start with making your progress charts on graph paper, listing the activities in order: math, clean the bathroom sink, phonics, clean the bathroom floor, geography, clean the bathtub (you get the point: alternate passive and active periods, academics and chores)—listed down the left side of the page. Now, go peel your potatoes right next to your child while he does math. Then have your child cross it off on his chart and move to the next thing listed—a chore.

Just begin...just begin...just begin. Just do five minutes in each subject for a week. Next week, increase it to 10 minutes. God is looking for beginners. He has an entire army of angels ready to dispatch to your side, the minute you show deliberateness in godly pursuits. I'm sure some of those angels just read newspapers; they end up hanging out and loitering about like aimless and listless vagrants until you purpose in your heart to reclaim Biblical ground. But when you take that first step, those angels perk up, drop their papers, whistle to each other, and step into action in your behalf. Do it in every area. If you're not in the habit of smiling, turn and smile at one of your children right now. If you need to be more cheerful, say some cheerful little thing right now. Begin. Start. Veer north.

All it takes is a resolute "want-to" to become a focused mother, teacher, and homemaker. That's all. Yet, the wellbeing of the next generation depends upon such a turn of the heart. **"Only engage, and then the mind grows heated. Begin it, and the work will be completed."**[1]

---

[1] Attributed to John Anster in a "very free translation" of Goethe's *Faust* from 1835.

Part 2:

How to *Train* Your Children, Not Just *Discipline* Them

There is almost no subject more important than learning how to train and discipline your children. You can't teach a thing to a child until you have his attention. I used to tell my student teachers that they grew up on one side of the  teacher's desk, but now they must come around to the other side. No matter how awkward it may feel, donning authority is a responsibility that God requires of you whenever you are in charge of children. Faithful, consistent attention to discipline will yield rewards for your family in eternity and peace in your home here and now.

Laying hold of parental authority is much like putting on a coat. A parent picks up the office of authority at first and then by and by grows into a wise, judicious use of it as it is exercised over the years. It is possible to be very calm and loving with one's children while at the same time exerting great authority. People have no doubt noticed extreme differences in athletic coaches. Some rule by tyranny, put-downs, and rage; others direct by a firm, controlled love. Napoleon said that Christ was the greatest of all conquerors because all the others conquered by force but Christ was the only one to do so by love.

Most colleges don't offer a course on how to discipline your children. They don't even offer one for education majors. Beginning teachers have to learn it around the campfire of experience working with hundreds and hundreds of children. I hope to spare you the 25 years it took me to master these principles so that you can acquire and use them by nightfall.

We're told in Scripture that Eli did not restrain his sons. No doubt Eli, being a godly man, spoke and pleaded with his sons, even to the point of cajoling them in his attempts to discipline them. He clearly wanted his sons to please God. But in the end, Scripture has this short, sad sentence to say: "he did not restrain them" (1 Samuel 3:13, NKJV). Eli did not see to it that his wishes were turned into actual behavior. He did not corral their flesh. He did not intensify the train-ing until it was accomplished and took root under his authority. His discipline was wind.

Submission of the flesh

The mother of a newborn asked a famous general, "Give me wisdom for my baby." He promptly replied, "Teach him to deny himself." The more you help your children to subdue their flesh, the less trouble they'll have with themselves later on. I had a friend in college whose parents were missionaries. Because they had trained her so well spiritually, she had no trouble being faithful with her daily devotions. She just woke up each morning, sat upright in her bed, grabbed her Bible and had devotions. I, on the other hand, had a terrible time forming the habit because I had not grown up with it. So, that's the kind of gift you give to your children (and their future spouses). The more you teach them to subdue their flesh while they are young, the better.

George Washington evidenced a rare degree of self-control, even at an early age. One time someone stepped up to his  mother and asked, "To what do you owe his greatness?" Without batting an eye she answered, "To his HABIT of obedience." He wasn't always in the valley of decision over every request that was made of him. He had formed the habit of setting his feet in the position to obey without a discussion first. This is the kind of man God picked to be the first president of the greatest country in the world. His degree of self-control worked for him a page in every child's history book.

Obedience should be instant and joyful. If your children respond with delayed obedience, what good is it? *Delayed obedience is disobedience. Obedience is the place of blessing.* These two sentences can be repeated aloud in the home often, to keep the family's goal crystal clear.

The obedience should also be cheerful. Think of Mary's response when she heard that she would carry the Son of God in her womb. She joyfully replied (Luke 1:38, 34, KJV), "Be it unto me according to Thy word. ... How shall this be?"

Zechariah asked the same question (Luke 1:18), but curtly and in disbelief: "Well, how could that be?" It was the same question, but asked in a different spirit. That humble entreating joyful spirit of Mary's issued in the *Magnificat*, a poetic song of praise that has been sung down through the ages. Zechariah, on the other hand, was struck dumb.

Submission requires strength. We have a perception in our culture that submission is weakness. It takes tremendous power to get yourself to do by obedience what you wouldn't choose to do right now, if it were left up to your emotions. Children who have learned self-control grow a secure self-image. Children who are out of control are miserable. They cry out for boundaries.

In *Foxe's Book of Martyrs* there is an account of a woman who was going to be burned at the stake for following Christ. On the day of the burning she asked the executioner,

"Would you please bind my cords tight?—because I fear my flesh." She knew there was a part of her that would want to walk away from that stake and not die for Christ, and she was, in effect, saying, "Tie me up tight so *that* part won't win."

Twelve persons beheaded or burned at Deventer in 1571.

Inform your children that there is this flesh in them that is ugly and we're going to subdue it. We're going to first acknowledge that it exists, and then we're going to subdue it so that you can rise above the seedy part of yourself for God, and so that you can be loved in the community.

Foxe's Book of Martyrs also describes a man who recanted his previous testimony that he was a Christian. He signed a form saying so—but he couldn't sleep that night. He realized he was weak, and he abhorred what he had done. The next day he went to the King and turned himself in, declaring, "I DO believe in Christ; do to me what you will." So he, too, was burned at the stake. On the site of his burning, however, he leaned down and stuck his hand in the flame first, saying "Any part of me that denied my God— I want to burn that first."

The ancients knew they had a flesh. The modern man doesn't know that. He hears slogans like…"You deserve a break today." We are swimming in self-indulgence in our culture. The old guys knew how to put themselves under for higher gains.

The more YOU help your children against their flesh now, the less they'll have to battle with themselves later. There is nothing sorrier than an adult who lacks self-control.

George Macdonald said it well, too, in his storybook, *The Two Princesses*. "Instead of making your daughter obey you, you left her to be a slave to herself. You coaxed when you ought to have compelled, you praised when you ought to have been silent, you fondled when you ought to have punished; you threatened when you ought to have inflicted—and there she stands, the full grown result of your foolishness!"

Begin with the end in view

As a parent, you want to begin disciplining with the end in view. What kind of person are you raising? Do you want a rigid, wait-on-me type of person, or do you want someone who displays a flexible, magnanimous spirit—someone who can accept most any circumstance.

If you want a rigid child, pander to his self-will. If you want a magnanimous spirit, you're going to have to cross that will, time and time again. You can explain that you are crossing their will on purpose, to help prepare them to be flexible at someone else's home or while camping out.

Your child should come to feel at home with self-denial, for the good of others. In the old film *The Miracle Worker* there's a dramatic scene where the teacher and her student are under the table, rolling on the floor while the teacher is trying to make the child fold a napkin. Remember the outcome? The teacher looked like a wreck when it was over, but Helen Keller submitted.

Why the big deal? Because the teacher knew that the outcome of that battle would affect all future interchanges. She knew that she *had* to win. So it is with your interchanges with your child. Many times you will enter into conflict with your child, and you *must* win in order to secure the respect of your child toward all the good that you have in mind for him in the future.

Consider another example from history. There was a time when Susanna Wesley was teaching her child something that she had to explain over and over. When she reached the seventeenth time her husband exploded with, "Why do you tell that child the same thing 17 times?" She answered, "Because if I didn't persevere to the 17th time, when the child finally

understands it, I would lose all of my beginning labors." That is the way discipline is accomplished—by steady uncompromising consistent effort to reach a desired end. Until the behavior yields to your pressure, the job is not finished.

We can see yet a third powerful picture of discipline in Shakespeare's play, *The Taming of the Shrew*. (Perhaps you can find the old black and white film.) It is a superb treatment of bringing someone's wayward will into submission. This is not a recommended strategy to use with your *spouse*, but it is an excellent strategy to use with your *children*.

The Taming of the Shrew is the story of a confident young man who got to choose between three young ladies for his wife. Two of them were rather demure; one was wretched. To everyone's surprise, he picked the wretched one—the lass who threw a temper tantrum every day.

But, strangely, he proved wiser than his friends knew. On the honeymoon, he cleverly proceeded to throw several temper tantrums himself, supposedly on her behalf, in the name of love, right before she did. When they entered the bedroom of their inn, for example, he pitched a fit FOR his beloved, ranting and raving that the mattress was not soft enough for her. "Off with it!" he shouted, "We will sleep on the floor instead."   She spluttered in confusion, saying timidly, "Well, I would have liked to have at least *tried* the bed."

At dinnertime he also threw a fit, declaring the food not fit for his beloved. He returned it to the kitchen. She again argued that she would have liked to have tried it.

At every turn, where there was a potential possibility of her foul spirit expressing itself, he jumped the gun and threw the fit himself.   Over the course of the honeymoon, this proved to show her the wretchedness of a disagreeable and contrary spirit. So much so, that on the way home when he saw the sun, he called it the moon, just to see whether she would agree with him. She protested mildly, saying that it was the sun. But when he declared it again to be the moon, she hastily dropped her contentiousness and agreed for the sake of harmony between them. It now didn't matter to her what the reality of the case actually was. She was now more interested in exhibiting a yielded spirit and achieving relational harmony than with asserting her own perceived rightness of the situation.

He arrived home with a much softened, sweet-spirited wife. He engaged his comrades (who had likewise married the other two in the meantime) in a wager to call their wives by whistle or by messenger. The husbands of these supposedly demure women found them subtly resistant after marriage. They did not come running when called—in fact, they *refused* to come. But the hero of our story now had a wife who agreeably appeared and surprisingly graced all who beheld her. This is the goal you want for your children: to train them to be agreeable and to have a magnanimous spirit.

How do you do it? You use the same strategy Shakespeare's character did. Let's say your children come to the dinner table and you give them plastic forks. One of the forks, however, has a tine broken off—and this distresses one of your children. Simply remove the fork entirely from your child's place. Then go to your kitchen drawer and pull out the biggest turkey fork you can find and give it to your child in place of the plastic one. You then say, "If you complain, your situation will always worsen. You will now eat with the turkey fork."

Let's run another scenario. Let's say all the children come to the table and there is a battle about which chair is best. It soon becomes apparent that one of the chairs is a bit rickety because one of its wooden legs is slightly shorter. If a child complains, you could promptly remove the chair entirely, and have him *STAND* all during supper.

You can do it with food, too. Parents say, "Oh, I *can't* have food battles with my children." Yes, you *can*! That's where obedience can begin. If a child complains about the broccoli, you take away the entire plate and only serve the broccoli (just a small "no-thank-you" helping of it). He must eat that before you return the remainder of the meal. It won't be very long before he won't tell you what he doesn't like. He won't even *hint* at it.

Don't shackle yourself with a huge three-month battle over the broccoli. Just give the child a "do-able" little bite. My daughter used to beg, "Could I just SEE my favorite food while I'm swallowing this other food, so I'll have my reward right before me?" The result? Now she'll even drink raw cabbage juice, and we can take her out to restaurants that offer international cuisine. Eventually children can be conditioned to receive all foods with thanksgiving. If they won't eat their dessert because you serve it to them on their dirty dinner plate, instead of a clean one, then they get no dessert at all. You get the picture. This is the kind of yieldedness you can get from your child if you start early, with the end in view.

After training a child by denying him a stubbornly sought creature comfort, immediately follow up with some extra tender loving care between you two, so your child clearly perceives that you have his best in view and are not just being difficult or arbitrary.

Middle managers of large corporations are almost always promoted for their refined people skills, and seldom for their I.Q. alone. No doubt, many of these managers began to learn those skills as youngsters. So, too, you are training your children to stand out in public life by carefully tending to this matter of requiring obedience and growing a magnanimous spirit.

3 images for viewing discipline:

Three mental pictures of the dynamic of training discipline will nail these points that we have been considering.

Image #1: The carrot and the pitchfork

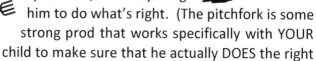

The first is of a carrot and a pitch-fork. You dangle the carrot of inspiration in front of your child and come along behind him with a "pitchfork," requiring him to do what's right. (The pitchfork is some strong prod that works specifically with YOUR child to make sure that he actually DOES the right thing in real life, during moments when the child isn't quite so sure whether he wants to obey or not.)

Storytelling is the carrot. During peaceful family times, saturate your child with stories of noble sacrificial heroes—both from the Bible and from history—as often as you can. But also use your "pitchfork" of reinforcement and forcefulness for ensuring proper behavior during rebellious sieges with your child. This combination of leading and prodding moves your little family flock into line. You'll be able to remind them of the noble stories during moments of discipline. One strengthens the other.

You could share episodes like these from Scripture:

❖ When God picked Noah to build His ark, Noah didn't respond with curt words. He didn't say, "Yeah, right, later, Lord." Or, "I'd rather use pine than gopher wood." No, the kind of man God chose was a man who was already in the habit of submission.

❖ God selected Mary to be the mother of Jesus because she had a certain quality of spirit about her. He didn't pick the local loud mouth/gossip.

Use these examples to show how God looks for prior episodes of self-control when picking men for his greatest exploits.

Also mention heroes from history, like Abraham Lincoln and Thomas Edison, emphasizing their self-denial. In addition to sharing these hero stories both from the Scriptures and from history, you want to heighten your child's awareness of specific character traits in general. There are nearly 50 character traits that your child can learn. God's character is perfect. Each time a person manifests some character trait in the way that he conducts himself, he glorifies God. Being punctual glorifies God. Exhibiting good follow-through with any project (sticking with the task until it is totally finished) glorifies God.

If you do not presently have a way to isolate each of these traits and teach them to your child, consider acquiring our *Character Traits Coloring Book and Songs Audio CD*. You can teach one trait a day until you've covered them all. Our approach is light-hearted and fun. It includes an object lesson (using some common household object for each one) and a catchy song of the core idea that they'll never forget. The coloring book ensures that you get the job done, because they color it, sing, it, and have it cemented in their spirits with an object lesson.

Teach these concepts in calm moments when anger or willfulness is not clouding their vision so that your children totally understand what the goal is. Then later you can refer to these concepts when their flesh is pitching a fit.

So, strive to raise *holy* children rather than academic children. You further accomplish this by irrigating and occupying their minds continually with holy material. Long ago one man said, "If I could control the books of the home, I could control the culture." Now, we'd have to add "control the media" to that. What goes into the mind WILL eventually be expressed in the life of the individual. So keep a guard at the gate of their minds.

See our titles *How to Cultivate a Lasting Love of the Bible in Your Children* (item #56 on our order form) and *The Two Most Common Pitfalls in Home Schooling* (#67) for a further discussion on this matter. Read scores of missionary biographies to your children when they are young, and when they're older have them read scores more themselves. It will do much to teach them self-denial. It will be as if someone else is continually training them, even when you are off-duty.

So, dangle the carrot of inspiration in front of your child through these heroes and character traits as frequently as possible, and, in addition, remember to come along behind with a "pitchfork" to make sure that self–discipline is worked out in the actual experiences of their little lives.

The inspiration insures that they are with you, on the same page, and that their desires have been shaped by high ideals. And the pitchfork insures that righteous habits are progressively established in the life, by parental pressure.

Image #2: Horses' reins

The second disciplining image is that of
horses' reins. Good discipline is like steering a horse. If you
just discipline using only one rein, the rein of sentimental
love, you'll be pulling that horse (child) right around in a circle while you say things like, "You adorable child. I just want
to feed you M&M's all day." You will certainly spoil the child
and produce nothing but embarrassment for both you and
the child.

Conversely, if you train using only the other rein of tight
discipline, saying, "You little wretch, you just stepped out of
the circle of sanctification, you have 40 laps to do, now do
30 more," you'll create hatred and disdain in the child.

Good discipline is having a strong grasp of both being FIRM
and AF-firming the child, thus correcting him, evenly. Holding the reins of training in balance will result in your child
trotting right off and making confident progress in maturity.

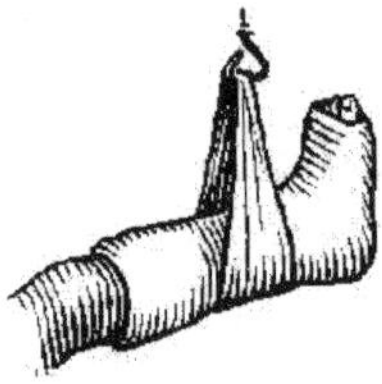

Image #3: Break and bond

The third disciplining image is called "Break
and Bond." You break the self-will, when
necessary, but you keep your eye on the big picture: that
you want to BOND with your children for a lifetime.

It is vital to remember that your children are interpreting
their childhood through their perception of what you're
doing to them. They will carry these perceptions with them
all of their life. You only get one shot at making memories
with your children. So if you are overly harsh, demanding,

and/or over-controlling, you may win the immediate battle but lose their hearts. To keep yourself balanced, ask yourself, "When they grow up, will they want to avoid me because I've been so tight on them—or will they delight to see me because I'm the most affirming, loving, person they have ever found to relate to?"

There's a payday coming for our parenting. It's a sobering thought. It's not meant to paralyze us but to season what it is that we're doing with our children now, and what kind of independence and affirmation we'll give them later, as autonomous adults.

It's important to cross the deviant will of a young child, yes, but it's also important to bond, to tie those heartstrings to you, to repeatedly tell your children how much you love them. You can never do too much of this.

Nurturing moments

Bonding with your children is accomplished by sharing many nurturing moments. "The wise woman looks well to the *ways* of her household" (Proverbs 31:27). This verse implies that she looks well to the progress of relationships within the home, not just keeping up with chores. It is possible to be so preoccupied with other matters when you're at home, that you're not really at home. Your children aren't receiving the benefit of your watchful, loving nurture. Strive to be an "all-there" mother who is responding to the needs of her children as they come up. Be a careful mother rather than a casual mother, in terms of thoroughly knowing the ways of your children.

In Malachi 4:6 the Lord says that in the latter days "I shall turn the hearts of the fathers to their children." Today it seems that when mothers are with their children, so often they, too, seem to their children to be far away. Knowing this, try to minimize other pre-occupations, simplify your life, and turn your heart toward your children as frequently as possible.

Be sure that your day includes many nurturing moments with each child. This is a time of deliberate focused attention upon each child. Your day's activities may not look any different, but the focus of your heart will be different. Deliberately pick out one child to lavish your love upon for a few minutes, while you work. Switch your focus throughout the day from child to child.

It works like this. While you do the laundry, set one child  upon the dryer and hand the clothes to him to dump into the washer. Smile on him, lovingly tell him a verse or sing a little hymn to him, jostle his knee affectionately, tell him what a good helper he is, and then set him back onto the floor and hold hands as you walk out of the laundry room.

Next, take another child with you to walk to the mailbox, tell her that God makes beautiful days as gifts for us, that clouds show us His glory, that God gave us to each other, and that God made her. Play follow-the-leader back to the front door, alternating who leads. Laugh. Tell her that she is so much fun to be with that you're glad that you belong to each other.

When you're mopping the floor, ask another child to be your cleaning buddy. Give him a damp rag to wipe the lower cupboards with or to wipe the floor right behind you as you go. Talk about how the children of Israel crossed the Red Sea. Make one side of the kitchen Egypt and the other Canaan. Work your way across the floor, talking about how wonderful it is to obey God, instead of drowning like Pharaoh and his army did. Tell him he is your forever friend. Smile lovingly at him, and kiss both of his hands when you've finished.

Or, sometime when you've come home from running errands, try crawling into the back seat to read a short book to your children and hug each one before asking them to help you bring in the groceries.

While you're cooking, include a child. Set her on the counter or on a stool standing next to you. Find some little thing for her to do, even if you have to do it over again later. Talk with her. Tune into just her. Really listen to what occupies her little heart. Don't just say "Uh, huh" while your mind is on something else.

Picture yourself as a bee, settling first upon this flower (child) and then upon that flower (child) all the day. Nurturing moments are priceless. Think of what it would feel like if someone had done that to you in your childhood. Don't you blossom, even now as an adult, under praise and attention?

If you'll take the time again and again to concentrate on these nurturing moments, you won't have a big relational mess to clean up in adolescence and you'll garner for yourself lifetime friendships with your own children. They will indeed rise up and call you blessed. Could you ever hear any sweeter words?

Raise up a shield of expertise in your child

According to psychologist Larry Crabb, every human being has two basic emotional needs: one is _to be loved_ and the other is _to matter_. We'll tackle the loved part at another time, in another parenting tip. But, for now let's tackle the "to matter" aspect.

Ever notice how a shy child forgets himself and blossoms behind a puppet? Young children need some skill or ability or talent out in front of themselves that helps define who they are until they grow older and more secure and can come out from behind the prop and "just be". We have become mature when we have learned to be comfortable with our own frail humanity—even if we've become old and can't do much. Children, however, aren't there yet; as they are emerging, they need concrete personal confidence-boosters to help them believe that they truly matter.

"Look mom, I can ride my bicycle without tipping over." "Look mom, I can slam dunk the basketball nine times out of 10"...are statements made behind a comforting shield of some external thing or achievement. What the child really says is, "Look mom, I am validated by what I DO! I matter! I'm a good artist, or a good walker of the dog. I'm a pianist. I'm a speech giver. I'm a gymnast." Give a child no shield to hide behind as he grows, and the social spotlight can burn badly, making him feel worthless. A child who is constantly on the raw end of negative comments such as jeering or ridicule for being a nobody can become suicidal later on, if that persecution continues long enough without something he can cling to that he does well.

Viewing your child only as an appendage to yourself is shortsighted. He must be given the tools to grow an independent capable strength of his own, in as many areas as possible. All through his childhood, you must be "for him", not he "for you."

As we mature, we all eventually discover that we are not just a football coach or a carpenter or the city clerk or a singer, or a good husband or mother. We are something that we can't quite comprehend, something beyond what are jobs are, somehow, someway made in the image of God. To understand that we were made solely FOR GOD (Isaiah 43:7) takes us a lifetime.

At first, it helps us to be the bicycle rider, to survive emotionally and psychologically. God Himself designed it this way. In fact, if truth be told, He, our Heavenly Father, steadies the back of the bike seat for us as we're getting underway.

C. S. Lewis wrote, "Lovers relate face to face, friends...side by side." Wise parents cultivate this "side by side" business as their children are growing up, while God slowly and deftly brings them face to face with Himself. It begins to dawn on the emerging adult that there was another hand on his bicycle seat.

Because "to matter" is such an important component of a healthy childhood, we, as parents, need to look for ways to

fan *some* flame in our child—many little flames, in fact—
even if it begins with applauding them only over being the
family's best table-setter or the best one to make the baby
laugh. Eventually we should aim to deliberately, systemati-
cally, and progressively develop more accomplished shields
as the child grows. Academics, domestic skills, talents, and
financial/ entrepreneurial skills all grow the child's real self-
esteem—a self-esteem that eventually is not dependent
upon any defining activity, but is secure enough to just "be".
Personhood has been established.

When your child is young, watch him carefully for clues
about what the hands-on skills and talents might be, because they begin to show themselves early on, even in tod-
dlers, if you are alert to them. Which aspect of a project
does he run to—the technical, the procedural, the oversight,
the advertising? Is he engineer material? a counselor-type?
musical? athletic? botanical? artistic? inventor-type?
writer-type, always picking the precise word rather than the
general one? scientific? dramatic? cooker? sewer? carpenter? organizational? Identify his tendencies and proc-
livities. Take careful note of his speedy agilities with certain
tasks.

When your family identifies a natural bent in your child,
early on, encourage it. Loudly praise it. Nurture it and provide for its development. Then, if you see it manifested
more and more, get him apprenticed in it. Build up the
shield and you'll build up the person behind the shield,
simultaneously. This is as vital to your child as food, clothing
and shelter. It will, in fact, help him survive, even without
the other three.

Can you love your child too much?

Now let's discuss Crabb's other point. Every human being has a need to "be loved". Can you over-love a child? No. It is impossible to over-love a child. It would be like saying of the Heavenly Father, "His love doesn't endure forever", and "He didn't keep His covenant of love with His people for very long" (this is *not* to be found in 2 Chronicles 6:14!).

When we talk about making your child "feel loved," we're talking about parenting with a *mature* love. It *is* possible to spoil your child by giving him too much materialism too early, by setting no limits and boundaries on his behavior, or by responding to his foot-stomping demands. In these  cases, withholding loving *feelings* and *actions* might be a deeper love, if it is needed to teach the child responsibility, and thwarts his self-absorption. Real love aims to lead the child to higher ground.

We're talking about a wise mature, 10-steps-ahead-of-them kind of love. This love prays for the child. This love anticipates and goes ahead of the child, laying out broader and broader wholesome opportunities for the child's own personal expansion. But also, this sort of love can be felt. A child so loved registers over and over again in his own small emotional accounting book that he has once again experienced real caring from his parents. This is a love that perhaps would:

- Occasionally stop and help your child hunt for something that is lost.

- Look in his eyes as he talks with you, and listen to him attentively.
- Smile warmly at him—often—as in, "all day", even soon again after he has irritated you.
- Ask him later, if he was able to figure out something to his satisfaction.
- Ask adolescents *feeling* questions, "How did that make you feel?" and "Do you want to talk about that?"
- Sing *with* a little one, and sing *to* him at bedtime.
- Read to him, especially Bible stories that are on his level, character building stories, and lots of missionary biographies. Almost nothing beats reading together for emotional warmth; the parent's droning voice coupled with the safe and secure side by side body touch is almost unparalleled as a vehicle for loving a child. Do massive amounts of this in the early years—massive amounts.
- Take daily walks with him. Occasionally join in hikes, and sports. Play board games that develop the mind, and are not based primarily upon chance: Chess, Scrabble™, Fictionary, and Password™.
- Include him in some part of your current project, with a little companion project, right next to you. Involve him in your work as much as possible, throughout the day.
- Pay him for extra jobs, to give him worth. The Bible says the workman is worthy of his hire. It affirms his dignity.
- Refrain from using your child as your slave. Make sure that your requests for him to do something for you are not excessive. As he grows older, limit these requests to what would be appropriate to ask of a spouse or another adult. Otherwise, the child will feel trapped under your constant demands, and will want to squirm to get away from you at the youngest age possible.

- Refrain from micromanaging him in his own little world of choices and desires. Don't overly rule him, in minutia, to his exasperation.
- Be his first paying customer in every childhood business, be it a lemonade-stand, car washing, or harvesting apples.
- Talk about him positively, aloud, within his hearing, in front of others. Never say things like "He is our problem child in this area" or "He has problems with..."
- Help him with some little further enabling to make him *more* successful with his own little project.
- Every once in a while, color in a coloring book page together with him. I have no idea why children enjoy doing this *with* a parent, but they seem to love it!
- Let your children teach *you* something from their music lessons, or teach you *anything*. Let them "lord it over you" in some innocent, fun way (maybe including tying up daddy with ropes—but make sure *mom* is un-tied, in case things get out of hand!).
- Put love notes on their pillows and mirrors, and in their food.
- Surprise your little girls by "tea and crumpets" just once in their childhood. (Make them dress up and stay in their rooms until you have it all ready for them.) Surprise your boys with go-carts or bumper cars of some sort, or arrange for them to scramble up in huge tractor trailers, or super tall machinery, or go for a ride in someone's private plane the next time they take it out for a spin. Or arrange for both your boys and girls to watch a veterinarian do surgery. You get the point: be conscious of filling their childhood with memories.

None of us will be perfect parents, nor did we ourselves have perfect parents. But look back in your own childhood at what your parents *did* do right and emulate that part.

Look there for clues. Ask further, of yourself, what did some other adult do to you, as a child, that made you feel really loved? Your grandparents? Your aunts and uncles? A kind neighborhood gentleman or lady? Your own friends? Recall what made you feel good and what currently makes you feel good, even now. Do all those big things to your own child, sometime. And do the little things every day. Fill up his love bank, and he'll love his parents back and go on to become a great friend of many others. He will have learned how to love, by experiencing it himself. Keep that love bank empty or skimpy and he'll flock to the approval of peers or the strange man hanging out at the corner lamp post.

Absolute surrender and lavish love

Keep your eye on the magnanimous grown adult you desire your child to become. Fashion him to that end. You simply must learn to love his soul better than his immediate wish, if it is not good for him. Cross his contrary willfulness with your own strong resolve, so that he is supple in your hand over every issue, having no will of his own, if it be contrary. *Absolute Surrender*, an 18th century book by Andrew Murray, says this is the goal of our own soul, as well: to withhold nothing from God—eventually coming to obey anything God would ask of us. As this is the goal of the mature soul with its Maker, it must be the goal of our parenting for the emerging fledgling soul, too. Seeing such a yielded, unselfish soul in any person is a beautiful thing, indeed.

Your child must perceive that you love him lavishly, so that he interprets all the aforementioned denial in the context of your ultimate good will and your desire to do what is best for him. Demanding only denial from your child will crush his spirit and your relationship. Remember that your job is to teach him not only self-mastery but also how to love, by his own experience of your own loving ways, surprises, warm smiles, cherishing his little stories, etc. Make it your goal to parent just like the Father does with you and you can't help but be right on target.

> Practice firmness in crossing his unpleasant bouts of self-will, but check yourself often for how much love you're expressing daily to your child. It's a sure combination.

Training, not tyranny

Parenting is not really very much about punishment at all; it is about training. Your goal is to **train** so well *ahead of time*, as well as thoroughly, *through and after each difficult moment,* that eventually your child will rarely need punishment at all.

Training involves actual practice session in the flesh.

Let's look more closely at building the foundation—what those practice sessions look like. Have as your goal, to take some time in small quiet moments (you *do* have some of these throughout your days), to raise the standard of acceptable behavior in your child's mind. When your child is peaceable, take that time to inspire, to describe, to practice what obedience feels like in the flesh—calmly.

A horse trainer puts his horses through the paces in private, before they encounter the spotlights and the distractions.

And after the young horses have been in the spotlights and he notes the weak areas, he brings them back to the practice arena again and again, to diminish what can go wrong in the spotlights the next time. He actually over-trains his beloved horses to ensure it won't go wrong. This is precisely what a professional musician does: practices like crazy, and then performs. Whatever passage falls apart under pressure gets hauled back to the practice room to give it "what for" once again.

Train your child to come to you at your first request in your own living room. Or your own backyard. Practice it. Practice it when he is happy. Give him a big reward at first. Praise him. Practice whispering the same command and getting the same obedient response. Then ratchet it up a level. Practice it when he starts getting absorbed in something else and doesn't want to. Practice it. Repeat it. Go over it again. The goal? First call, instant response, cheerful attitude every time. Don't quit until this is engraved into his autonomic nervous system, and he knows you mean business.

Now this is the anatomy of a training session. This method can be used to obtain obedience in any area. It can be done over what to eat, what to wear, how to do a chore, how to sit in a car-seat, how to not talk when a guest IS talking, etc., over 1,000 points of a civilized life. Here are the steps:

Training step #1: First of all you have a nice quiet talk about all the people who do this attribute splendidly, in your current life, among relatives. If it's applicable, you can also point out historical and biblical characters who were models of exemplary behavior.

Training step #2: Then ask a few questions. "When Daddy sits in the car and buckles his seat belt, does he thrash about or scream? Have you ever seen Daddy scream, putting his seat belt on? Have you ever seen Julie's daddy, down the street, do that? Do *you* want to still be screaming when you are a daddy, over such a little thing as a car seat? Have you ever seen your mom throw her food? Have you ever seen Aunt Tizzy slam her book down? Have you ever seen Uncle Harry hit and bite your grandmother!!! Barking dogs do these things, not people!

"Now, because you chose to scream, or chose to throw something in the house, you will now face the consequences, so that you can make better choices next time."

Training step #3: Finally, practice what obedience feels like in the flesh.

If the child protests over anything you ask him to do, you make sure and have him do a little bit more of the thing he just protested about—until he can do it peacefully without the protest. You surprise him with this outcome *later*, not during the crisis. Just get through the crisis. Then later in the day have a quiet talk, "You know when I asked you to do such and such, earlier in the day, you threw a little fit. I just want you to clearly understand that every little fit will always cost you something—even if you don't see the results right away. Unpleasant results *will* eventually happen to you, every time, so now:

...because you threw a fit over the shoes or shirt I asked you to wear today, you will wear them again tomorrow—and if you throw an additional fit right now over *that* news, you will be wearing them again the next day.

...because you threw a fit when you got in your car seat before we went to town, I will now bring the car seat in the house and set up the sand timer next to it and you will sit in the car seat until the sand runs out (just a minute or two) quietly, and if you have trouble with that little task, we will do it again, when you least expect it and when you are happily trying to do something else.

...because you threw a fit over the lima beans, you will now have *only* the lima beans, before you will receive anything else to eat." Make it a policy that at every meal, initially **serve only a tiny portion of everything**. You can always dollop on seconds, and thirds later, after they have eaten the little bit of everything. You will waste next to no food this way. Families who don't adopt this plan, early on, with all of their children, with all food, waste unspeakable amounts of food and money, feeding their trash cans.

Meet each protest with a protest of your own—a quiet dignified one. Every time. If your goal is to train up a magnanimous adult and not a rigid willful one, you've got to train IN the flexibility, adaptability, and suppleness, and train OUT the habit of the quickly formed smoldering storms. Practice training **sessions** help get you down that road.

~~~~~~~~~~~~~~~

Now let's look at some practical, specific **tools** for child training.

Training tools

Just as a carpenter wears a tool belt, to have the appropriate tool close at hand, ready to use, depending upon the immediate need, so, too, parents need a variety of discipline/training tools. The first is one of prevention.

Training tool #1: Busy children are happy children

This first suggestion is guaranteed to dramatically cut down on your disciplining load as a whole. I learned it from a teacher who was so well loved that parents put their children on a waiting list years ahead of time to be sure to get them in her class when they came of age. Her slogan was "Busy children are happy children!" If you habitually run ahead of your children to plan for activities that will occupy them productively, you'll simply not have as many discipline problems to cope with. Knowing this, the teacher ended each evening at school by putting a fun, independent worksheet on each desk for the next morning. In addition, throughout the day the children were always presented with a variety of different activities to choose from whenever they finished early. They were never idle.

Planning your children's activities may involve some preparation on your part, either the night before or early in the morning, but you'll find that the more you prepare, the smoother your day will run.

Children get into trouble when they have nothing to do. You can just count on it. Mothers who take a shower or go run errands without first assigning activities, academics, or chores to do are setting their children up for deviant behavior and failure. "Idleness is the devil's playground." Children need something to do. To continually take things away from small children (because they are causing trouble with those objects) but not substitute something else more constructive to play with is not fair to a child. Their world of play is like your world of work. They problem-solve, experiment and role-play. They are not just going to sit and twiddle their thumbs. Letting a child use up a whole roll of clear plastic tape in the back seat of a car on a long trip, for example, might be bothersome to you, but it can't be that much trouble, and it gives the child something to DO. Reevaluate: is the child's activity causing real trouble or is it just inconvenient to you. Say yes to all you can. If you could use more ideas like these, get our *Training Terrific Tots* booklet for a look at 50 additional quick and wholesome activities to occupy preschoolers.

Keep your children so busy that they don't have time to become bored or depressed. After homeschooling in the morning, have your children focus in the afternoon on building their own home based business, and developing a good well-rounded exercise program of stretching, weight training and aerobics. (Contact us about ordering a soft-bounce rebounder. Discount store brands are all HARD bounces. Rebounders are terrific because they use up a lot of excess energy indoors during inclement weather. Mom, too, can exercise on them without ever leaving her children.)

Your objective is to provide open-ended afternoon activities that your children can become more and more skilled at performing. Running a little business, be it detailing cars (an excellent home based business for junior highers, see our *Drive 'n Shine* booklet for an accelerated way to start!) or mowing lawns, or selling bread and pies, or growing vegetables to sell, all teach valuable life skills. Pay your children from an early age for extra household jobs anytime they desire to work. It is some of the best money you'll ever spend. Get them building their little financial empires early, working toward a real life goal. You, as the parent, can do much to teach them that solid increase comes little by little, by having a job available to them at any time they want one. (It will be some of the best help you ever pay for, because you have taught such good work skills in your children that they'll outwork any outsider you could ever hire.)

Another excellent open-ended activity for the afternoon is to teach your children to touch-type 60 to 90 words a minute. If this is one of your goals for your child, there is no faster way to get the job done than with our Zoom-Type program. (It was developed because all of the other programs were too slow.) It only takes five days and they can begin as young as age six. After that, they continue to grow their speed, the more they practice. This is a lifetime skill that can land your older child a part-time extra-money computer data entry job, because he will be able to type faster than most of the competition.

Music practice is another open-ended activity. If you don't want to have to drive anywhere for expensive lessons, our Quick Piano course can give your child a superb foundation in piano, right at home, for just the cost of one lesson—and you don't have to take them anywhere. The course begins with chords and gives them a big sound fast. It is the only program taught almost exclusively with pictures. Once they get the basics down on piano, they can move on to acquiring proficiency on other instruments. Playing the piano offers the best foundation for all future musical training.

Staying ahead of your children with meaningful activities, be it coloring when a toddler, or building a model in junior high, keeps the home atmosphere positive rather than spending the day only putting out behavioral fires. Planning independent projects for your child means peace for you.

Wasting adolescence is a modern tragedy. It has resulted in poor self-image, boredom, depression and suicides. It was not always so. Our homeschool how-to booklet #48, *How Not to Waste Your Youth,* shows how, in contrast, many of our forefathers used their adolescence for maximum productivity. Benjamin Franklin had his own business up and running by the time he was 24. And (reversing those numbers) by the age of 42 he had multiplied his publishing business to other cities. He became independently wealthy, enabling him to go on and become a public servant. Many modern adults can't get beyond their own financial survival BASICS, because they didn't get serious dealing with real life early enough.

When they are young, keep your children busy with activities. When they are older, keep them busy with entrepreneurial enterprises, mentoring, exercising, practicing classical music, and speed typing.

Bottom line: busy children are happy children.

Training tool #2: Spanking

A second tool on your carpenter's belt is the use of an occasional, wise, "in control" spanking. The Bible calls it "using the rod." Let's stop a minute here to discuss this controversial topic. The world says, "Don't you dare lay a hand on your child to spank him." But some of those same parents quietly kill their own children in their wombs through abortion. And with the children they *do* give birth to, some parents wait so long to correct them that their children's indulged misbehavior makes the mom or dad erupt in yelling and shaking and eventually hitting their children in anger.

No wisdom has ever superseded that of the Bible. The Bible speaks of a training rod: a switch that delivers a shallow sting but does not hurt the child—a switch used to subdue willful rebellion in a child. A spanking is not a beating. This tool becomes the "board of education" on the "seat of knowledge" for your child, when young.

Use this switch, instead of your hands, at all times, even if it is inconvenient to go get it. Hands are for loving and should never be used to thump your child, flick your child, slap his face, knock him, or shake him, etc. When your hands approach your child they should always be associated with administering kindness, use only the rod for correction.

Here is what one Scripture verse says: "Because sentence against an evil deed is not executed speedily, therefore the hearts of the sons of men are fully set in them to do evil" (Ecclesiastes 8:11). In other words, spank [sentence] the child speedily [quickly, right after the infraction] so that the child doesn't become set in his ways to repeat his evil deeds.

If you don't administer correction to your child, his little wayward spirit grows up to become a big wayward spirit, determined to do evil. Reserve the rod for blatant, direct defiance of your authority, not for small irritations, accidents, immature oversights, etc.

Some naive parents don't think it is appropriate to spank their children—even if they fear their children are eventually headed to prison.

Let's digress a minute and talk about our modern prison experience. Sadly, even then, prison sentences prove ineffective. Biblical restitution (working hard to pay back the injured people) is simply not practiced in our modern penal system. Today there is little connection between the crime and the punishment. Inmates in "correctional facilities" often do leather-crafts and watch violent TV. Many don't even engage in hard labor on work crews building roads, for example, that could benefit the society.

Prison becomes a luxury vacation to some, costing more than it does to send a person to Harvard or Yale. We've lost our focus because we've put man's ideas above what the Bible clearly says.

Some parents who don't paddle their children for deviant behavior find that they can't take them out in public for the first 10 years of each child's life because they have no idea when their child will erupt—when they will become a menace to any public function and an embarrassment to their parents. Often these parents become enslaved to their children's inconstancies and are trapped by their children's tantrums.

Out-of-control children provoke adults to become out of control. More and more severe measures are taken by parents to curb wilder and wilder behavior. Spank, in control. If you're out of control, don't do it. One godly woman quipped, "I administer frequent small paddlings to prevent myself from abusing my child!"

As a further example of parental self-control, I knew of a mother who had seven children. She spoke so sweetly to her children I remarked about it one day asking, "Have you always been this gentle to your children?" She said, "Oh no, I trained myself. If I lost voice control and spoke harshly to the children, I would take myself into the bedroom, get down on my knees and repent. Then, I'd discipline myself by going without lunch. That would make me think twice before speaking harshly to the children again." When I shared that strategy with a mother of four children she said, in her dry wit, "If I did that, I'd starve!" The mother of seven was a Rhodes Scholar and was accustomed to self-denial. That kind of personal discipline is exemplary to us all.

Using the rod consistently when needed, like a switch upon a horse, is the Biblical tool for training. The best way to avoid anger is to spank on the first offense, swiftly and calmly. The wise use of it is the fastest way to clean the air and restore fellowship.

If you have to say, "You're going to get spanked" over and over, all you are doing is convincing yourself. If you have to say it once, then it is needed. Just do it, instead of saying it, and you'll have to do it less. Let's examine *why* we say, "You're going to get spanked!" instead of actually doing it. We make the idle threat to buy time for ourselves when it is inconvenient to stop what we're doing and administer the spanking. We're thinking we can just finish this phone conversation, read this page in our book, write this line, or finish stirring this cake mix. Just get used to it: disciplining children is always going to be inconvenient. It's part of having a vigilant, well-disciplined spirit ourselves to make it top priority worth putting aside our own convenience.

Prepare your children ahead of time to behave well in public. Tell them they should never, never act up or disobey in public, and that if they do they will get sure discipline at home. Then, if they do act up in public, take them home *right then*, discipline them, and then promptly bring them back out to that public setting—to the store or wherever you were—and again ask for the desired behavior. You should be able to just whisper this time and have your word obeyed. Abruptly taking a child home is so mortifying and embarrassing to the child that you probably will only need to go all the way from a store and back just *once*.

When some mothers try to spank their child, it turns into a free-for-all. They descend into having to chase the child around the house, up onto the beds and down, up onto the couches and down, to even catch the child. Then the young arms flail about so wildly that the mother cannot even find the child's seat to administer the discipline. Here's the remedy. In a quiet moment, explain to your child that sometimes he needs correction because he has chosen to rebel. Explain that when he chooses to disobey and step over the line, there will be a consequence. So, he knows that when he makes a bad choice he will experience a swift sting. That way, you have prepared him for what is to come and there are no surprises. Explain to him that when that time comes, you want him to bend over the bed or couch and tuck his arms in front of him, so that his hands won't get hurt during the switching. Practice this posture. With this preparation you should be able to give a tame, controlled spanking. If you are out of control, wait; you can still give that spanking an hour later.

When children get switched on their seat, where it is padded, they are to cry *quietly*. They are not to scream and carry on. Defiant children scream loudly when they are being justly punished to intimidate the parent. Do not allow it.

If you don't see a repentant spirit—if the child has grown angry, crossed his arms, or stomped out of the room—bring him back and administer another one until you see a truly repentant countenance. If spanking inflames him and makes him angry, then you haven't conquered his defiance. The job is not done. Your child is still in control of the atmosphere of your home, not you. And that creates chaos.

When all is over, require the child to come to you and say, like George Washington was required to do with his parent, "Thank you for correcting me." Follow up on the training an hour later by making another request, to see whether the attitude is indeed changed or whether it will all flair up again.

Remember, however, that when we're raising children there are many small infractions, accidents, immature oversights, carelessness, out-of-sorts moments, etc., that do not warrant a spanking and can easily be handled other ways. Reserve spanking only for cases of direct defiance.

For lesser issues often just a simple writing exercise will iron things out. If the child is old enough to write, write down what he did and what he should have done, allowing space between each line for him to copy what you have written. Writing helps clarify the issue and is an important part of training. Then require him to do the correct behavior. Don't hug and love and restore fellowship, etc., until the required behavior is completed.

Training tool #3: Divert attention

You don't have to meet everything with your child head-on, or take everything to the mat. Often you can overshadow their cantankerousness with something positive. You can replace a problem object with something less dangerous, by your own sheer enthusiasm for something else. You can artfully draw their attention away from their present vexing situation to something else. Isn't this ultimately the way adults learn to control their own anger, or their own vexing situations? They have learned the art of wrenching their own thoughts away to something more wholesome or life-giving, until the storm passes and they can get more mature perspective and objectivity on the situation.

Training tool #4: Make it counterproductive to them

Instead of making your children's misbehavior always seem like an irritation directly to you personally, make it known that such behavior really is counterproductive to the child's own self-interest. Pit him against himself, or his peers, or other family members—not always in relation to you. Say things like, "Your loud voice is irritating to your grand-parents. I'm sure they'd prefer a quieter voice." Or, "You are going to upset your friends if you act like that."

When he/she's in a disgruntled mood, don't answer them until they answer with a better tone of voice. If he/she is impatient, move more slowly. If he/she is whining, don't listen. Teach your child that their disagreeable attitudes will only slow down their own progress.

Training tool #5: Consistency

Have you ever noticed how invariably inconvenient it is to discipline your child? It happens when you're preoccupied, on the phone, etc. But God is training you in vigilance. Consistency is the name of the game. The more consistent you are in those early years, the easier your life will be later on.

The matter of turning out respectful individuals who are devoid of ungodly rebellion is more important than teaching academics. Stop and take time to train out the rebellion, even if it means you have to cut the quantity of math problems in half for that day. Training obedience is tops on your curriculum list, no matter what hour of the day.

If you note a rebellious spirit in your child on *any* point, even though other areas are compliant, know that the child is rebellious still. "Rebellion is as witchcraft and is an abomination" (1 Samuel 15:23a). You simply *must* counter that resistant spirit whenever and wherever it crops up. Keep in mind that the devil wants to defeat you in this matter. He will seek to do it by eroding your resolve. If he can wear you out in the beginning, he knows that he will reap all of your subsequent mature fruit, too—just as with abortion: when he kills the child, he kills the mature adult. By abortion of the fetus, he takes out the adult inventor, the artist, the chemist, too. So, stick with it, even if it feels like an inordinately long process.

Christopher Columbus's men, when out of patience and angry, nearly forced him to return to Spain when he was just three days from American soil. Think of what the world would have lost, had he given up. Often with a stubborn child a parent is tempted to cry out, "How long, oh LORD, how long?" The answer? Ephesians 6:13: "Having done all, to stand." Stay vigilant. Often we're tempted to change strategies with a really resistant child, or back down, when simple endurance is all that's in order. If a bird keeps hitting his head against a glass door, eventually he'll stop. Make yourself into an immovable wall for the resistant child, so that he comes to fully understand that his rebellious spirit NEVER gets him anywhere.

When training or disciplining you may need to provide episodes of rest or encouragement for a tired or weepy child, or to cut the chore or assignment in half for right now—but later, pick up right where you left off and continue until the child totally finishes the job, and or shows a change in attitude.

Do not cave in to a child who cries easily. Be unmoved by the tears or you'll wind up with an emotionally weak adult, who will seek to manipulate people by their emotions throughout the rest of their life.

Training tool #6: Re-runs

Let's look at another tool on your child training carpenter's belt: the use of re-runs. Let's say your junior higher comes home, slams the door, does not greet your guest, and sulks on his way upstairs. Require your child to do a re-run of his entrance the proper way. Have him go outside again, enter and quietly shut the door, greet your guest, and proceed upstairs cheerfully. By having to re-do the behavior, he will feel the difference in his body. Even if he tries to ignore your words, he'll soon wonder why he had to repeat his entrance, and that visceral learning will be more effective than any lecture from you, no matter how well crafted. Repeat the re-run until the desired behavior is achieved. He'll get tired of having to physically respond over and over. Most of the time when we discipline, WE TALK WAY TOO MUCH. Action is what is needed. Even just walking over to your child and firmly staring at him will get him to change his behavior.

One time, students entered my classroom after recess and one clumsy child spilled a potted plant off the desk. The other children made fun of the awkward child. I halted that scene and required a re-run. We put the plant  loosely back in the pot, and returned the pot to the desk. Then I said, "Let's all enter the room again, let Fred re-spill the pot, and this time the rest of you will stoop to help him pick it up and cover his embarrassment by your kind words." The re-run helped the children *feel* the desired behavior. Discipline is not about punishment; it's all about training.

Training tool #7: Shape the attitude

Training *actions* is only half the battle, however. Training *attitudes* is the heart of the matter. The secular schools cannot touch this area. They can require a modicum of exterior behavior for socialization purposes, but they cannot go after the heart. This is a critical area for you at home, because rebellion begins in the voice. Take note of the hostile voice and each slight sullenness. This early detection will help you to land on the small offenses so that the child won't even attempt the larger offenses.

When I was teaching, I told my students at the beginning of the year that they were to receive their academic training with gratefulness. I told them that in many countries, children don't have the privilege of getting an education. I informed them that complaining and grumbling would have no place in my classroom.

One day another teacher came to visit me in my classroom. Before talking with her I asked the students to take out their math books. I saw out of the corner of my eye that a girl grumbled. I asked the teacher to wait a minute, then addressed the student and told her to go stand in the hall. The other teacher looked shocked and asked what the student had done. I said, "She had a rotten attitude." The teacher responded, "You discipline for *attitude*?" I replied in the affirmative and then suggested that she behold the rest of my class. She did. They all smiled demurely back at her. Point won. You *can* gain the attitude that you require from your children. Raise the bar high. The better one's *attitude* in life, the higher one's *altitude* will soar.

If you have commanded something and your child obliged but made you pay for asking him to do it by filling your home with his rotten attitude, you're not there yet. A child uses a rotten attitude in the hopes of intimidating you into not asking him again. Somehow he knows that if he can make life uncomfortable enough for you, you may back down. If you find yourself not making certain requests because you don't have the energy for the storm you know will follow (or the grumping and complaining), you've been intimidated. Barrel through; force unpleasant encounters to happen until you are no longer intimidated on any matter.

Even if his attitude improves when you confront him, go ahead and administer the discipline you had in mind for the bad attitude he *already* displayed. Otherwise, you'll be swimming in a turbulent sea of manipulation over the momentarily improved attitude, without punishing the past attitude that was wrong.

If the child complains about a chore, double it. If they complain about academics, add on a little bit more—not enough to wear them out, but enough to let them experience the high cost of complaining.

Semantic atmosphere

A mom's ongoing running commentary is as vital to the success and atmosphere of the home as the very air that the family breathes. It is spiritual oxygen to the home, even if they live in a dark, dank basement in shanty town in a third world country. A mother can make a veritable heaven of any home, simply by the choice of her words. For a few

short years, what she says, IS! She shapes reality for the entire family via her tongue. The mother's words become the
air in which the children's kites can soar.

Children look up into their mother's mature face to know
how to view nearly everything—even a thunderstorm. If
you bundle a child up, and go out *into* the storm with joy,
you'll shape your child's view of storms for the rest of
his/her life. Just sit in a chair during a lightning storm with a
huge umbrella over the both of you, hugging each other
tightly, and say to the child "Isn't this *fun*?!
(smooch) "Oooooh, did you see *that* one?!"
(lightning). "Here comes another fantastic crack,
snarl, whip of a sound (smooch)...are ya' ready?...this is
gonna be exciting!" (smooch) "Whee!...Did you feel that
thunderbolt under our chair?! Are you feeling the wind in
your face yet?!" (smooch, smooch). Then move on to
storms of a different nature.

For a great while, you interpret life to them as it happens.
The children both see the event and hear your running
commentary. The children watch you for how to interpret
setbacks and hardships, how to interpret and handle difficult
relationships, what spin to put on most every happening.
Your own daily off-the-cuff editorials end up being far more
influential than your children's textbooks. Your running
commentary is teaching on the backstroke, but more formative than anything deliberate, calculated or practiced. Most
parents are oblivious to these lessons that they teach.

Yes, a loving mother can put a positive spin on absolutely
everything: sub-zero weather, an out of sorts spouse,
poverty, handicaps, a broken chair, or even a bout with the

chicken pox. One such mother told her child, when he suddenly came down with chicken pox, that they were going to have a chicken pox party! She fixed popcorn, read stories, sang songs, counted the chicken pox, gave wonderful candlelight baths, rubbed soothing healthy lotions on, and three days later when the child said, "Mom, I don't want to do a chicken pox party, anymore," the worst had already passed.

When a chair breaks, for example, a cheery mom can say, "Oh goodie, let's turn the chair upside down and learn how to be "fix-it" people! It is so fascinating to see how things are made, or function, and apply our brightest minds to figure out how to fix them!" My father-in-law loves to fix things; we all gather around and watch him tinker (while he softly hums), because he makes it so much fun to conquer things.

The world you create with your tongue builds a child's heart, perspectives, appetites, and attitudes. It fortifies him with courage, ennobles him with purpose, and spurs him on with aspirations. Semantic atmosphere can tear a child down or emotionally resurrect him. It is hemoglobin for the mind and heart. What is said in the day swirls in and through a child's psyche, even while he sleeps.

You have the world by the tail for a few short years. Are you the shrew in the grocery store, or an angel from heaven? Shakespeare said, even of just the mere sound of a woman's voice: "Her voice was ever soft and low—an excellent thing in a woman!" Watch the quality, tone, and sound of your every word, as if you're pouring concrete for the foundation of a huge castle. And then be conscious of choosing the finest crystal and gold for your actual words. Never forget that you are building castles in the air, and an irreversible childhood on the ground. God gave you permission to do it. And you'll never again have such a carte blanche chance to do it for anybody, ever.

To build such an uplifting semantic atmosphere, you can use words like, "You're my sunshine; I delight in you." Using these sorts of words, even on days when you don't feel like saying them, is like erecting the wooden forms for wet cement. Love will rush into our forms and will set up like concrete, to stay. Remember, "The wise woman builds her house" (Proverbs 14:1). You do most of that building with your tongue. (You can change the semantic atmosphere even within your own head, by redefining your discipline troubles as disciplining challenges or opportunities, instead. Your changed thought-life will immediately lighten your load.)

Anytime you are working your children hard, give them a vision for it in a larger setting by regularly referring to a bigger picture. Get them to higher ground with your cheer-leading words. Here are some examples:

- "Just think: when you have finished reading the entire Bible all the way through, you will have read more Scripture than 99 percent of all the adults in our entire state!"

- "When you get done learning how to do this you can completely run a _____ business! You'll be the youngest person in the country to know how to do this."

- "Just think: when you have to do this as an adult, you won't have to learn how to do it then! You'll already know how, and will be free to show others how to do it. You'll be the expert everyone else will need and will look to."

• "When you can do *this*, the neighbors' jaws will drop."

• "Someone will observe your character and your skill and go tell somebody. In no time you're gonna be wanted by customers from miles around."

• "After all these mistakes this year with this project, you will be that much ahead of everyone else who are only just starting to learn these things next year. You are right up there with Edison, man!!!"

A mom's applause can get children to the moon and back. They soar on your words and the bigness of the future—and hearing about their significant place in it. Visualizing themselves as leaders, whom everyone is hanging on, gives them the grit to do what has to be done today. It gives them an edge of confidence and competence unequaled from children who grew up without such applause. It is an awesome thing to build a triumphant atmosphere in your home, regardless of any seemingly defeating circumstances, just this way, sentence by sentence.

If possible, work with your children in all their endeavors, so they will know you're united as a team and are not indifferent to their efforts.

Whether it be learning to change a tire or cracking an egg, parents provide the forward inspiration to it with their words. "We will now crack the whole dozen eggs so that we progress at mastering this skill. We'll get so that we can do this with no egg on the floor, no shell in the dish. We'll chip away at it this morning and again tomorrow morning and the next until it is conquered—and you become positively amazing at cracking eggs (or tying shoes, etc.). The parent visualizes the fledgling first attempts at all skill areas as they will be when the skill is fully mature and needed in the adult world. The parent transfers this vision of the end result to the child now as a means to motivate him or her.

You say to your seven-year-old: "We will learn how to make this oatmeal!" (It is a difference between the child sloppily doing work only for the present, and bothering the parent...to, instead, tackling the skill with gusto, and it becoming an art form, a challenge to do it skillfully: putting his heart into the skill and his rolled up sleeved arms into the effort.) "We will learn how to make this oatmeal well and make it earlier than others, to the end that we will then be able to help the world in this area as soon as possible."

The parent saturates today's otherwise "boring" skill, math problem, piano practice, writing challenge, etc., with comments like: "I know a mother of ten who still can't make oatmeal well. You will do it excellently. You will pay attention to the details. You will be a marvel. You will be able to help the family down the street when the mother is ill. You will be capable." By your words you transfer the thrill of becoming capable in as many things as you possibly can bring under your child's dominion!!! The parent's job is to transfer to the child an **appetite** for the finished **ability**. Both parent and child wind up immensely happy at every undertaking, if it is done in this spirit.

| The key: | They grill the steak; you add the sizzle. |

Why thank-you

As we've seen, your child needs your words of affirmation. You, on the other hand, can easily live without your child's words of appreciation. You don't *really* need them. Why, then, would you require them? Why does God require them? Perhaps you've at one time secretly wondered why the God of the universe requires praise of Himself. Is He an egomaniac? Surely not. We get a surprising answer to this seeming incongruity in God's character by reading the Psalms. "Praise becomes the righteous" (Psalm 33:1). Here we see that God requires such adoration because it looks good on US! It is good for our hearts to be subdued before a Holy God. Humility is our best side. It is beautiful dress upon us. The praise of Him turns out to be for our sake. Who but the God of the universe could have designed such a paradox?

So, too, you don't wield authority over your children for your own sake. You require it of them simply because saying thank-you looks good on THEIR faces. Reverence and respect for others is good for THEIR hearts. Your requirements are not those of a tyrant; they are born of benevolence, if we are the LORD's.

The authority of your word

Learn to take your own word of authority seriously. When your children are young, spend lots of time following up your own word—giving it weight. This will result in having it take almost no time later; your authority will have been established.

When you say something to your children, you must believe it yourself, first. Ask yourself, "How important is it that my own word be obeyed?" If you take it laxly, your children will take it laxly. If you think of it merely as a suggestion and not as a command, your children will respond just that way—and will avoid even the suggestion. If you can be talked out of it, or if you believe, after experiencing some resistance, "Oh, that request didn't really matter anyway," your children will adopt the same attitude.

If you take up your children's counter-suggestions instead of your own original command, they will become entrenched in offering those alternative suggestions—and demanding them. If you become preoccupied with something else after issuing your command, your children will do the same. If you answer their question of "Why?" they will ask it every time. If you condescend to discuss it, you'll go to bed with discussions and wake up with discussions—as chains about the ankles of your every command. Children are little lawyers lookin' for loopholes. Don't even start to answer their whys.

Never ask children why they committed an infraction. They don't know why. It's the old cursed sin nature. Ask instead, "What did you do?" and "What should you have done?" If they can't answer, or don't know, you tell them, and have them repeat it to you. Don't go there, or you'll find they have quickly gotten you out of your boxing ring into theirs, right where they willfully want you. If they respond slowly, or not at all (with one eye cocked on your response), they'll get the message that you are okay with that.

It is very inconvenient to have to follow your own word around the house to see that it is done—your every word to them. Nevertheless, in the beginning with every child you must **hover over your own word** until it is executed—each and every time. You can do this without a further word, after your first command. Stare at them. Go put a hand on their shoulder and point them in the right direction. Go just stand next to them. Tower over them and don't move. Command them even just with your firm eye, afterwards, merely looking in the direction you want them to go.

You must learn to **become vigilant over your own word.** The project you'd rather be doing at the moment is not your highest priority—the soul of your child is. **God is training *you* in the diligence of authority. You'll have to get over your own sluggishness— your weakness in not wanting to have to battle again.** This is hard work. At first it is exhausting. Yet, all valuable pursuits and ambitions in life are hard-won, if they are worth anything. This is no different. Buckle up. "There is a cost for doing something and a cost for doing nothing." The cost for *not* believing in your own authority is domestic chaos and being ruled by your children. If your children are not obeying you, they are ruling you. Not only are you not lord of your home, God is not Lord of your home—your *children* are.

Conversely, remember that you are not raising personal servants or slaves. The result of *that* could well be that when they are grown they may want to maintain a protective distance from you. Make sure that the motive of all your commands is to have a peaceful, loving home life that is running smoothly, and that your commands are ultimately for their sake, for their own maturity, not for your own self-indulgence or your every whim. At some deep level, your children will know the difference. Dictators throughout history often have hard final chapters they hadn't counted on.

Respect, and appeals to authority

Sometimes you're out of it. You're cranky. You've had a hard day running errands or dealing with a relative who is ill, and you find yourself requiring some crazy thing from your child. Your child recognizes it's crazy or undoable, or sees that it conflicts with something else. What should he do? Teach your child how to appeal to authority. Prepare him ahead of time by discussing this principle and tell him that you want him to put his feet in the direction of obeying by starting to obey, making it evident that he *will* do whatever you asked of him. Tell him that while he's headed to obey he may appeal your authority with a reverent and humble heart. For instance, your child may say, "I'd be glad to do that thing for you, Mom, but I didn't know if you were aware that Dad just said the opposite. Would it be all right if I don't?" Or he can say, "Would it be all right if I did it later? I'm still mowing the lawn and I don't want to have to start the mower again, but I'd be happy to do it right now, if you'd prefer." Such phrases express the proper spirit of an appeal. They are not whining or saying "Why should I?" or "Mom just said the opposite."

If you say "It is time to come to supper" and your daughter yells back "Just a minute, I want to finish this one thing," let her know that that response is not permissible. She is to say instead, "Yes, sir [or ma'am]. May I finish just this one more thing, or do you want me to come right now?" Once this posture of respect is heard in the voice, you can often let a child stay and complete their task for a few minutes more. We can train our children to act like Daniel did in the lion's den when he said, "Oh King, live forever." He treated his king with reverence, even when he was being unjustly treated in a lion's den.

Some day your child may need to make this sort of a gracious appeal to his boss or to his spouse. "I'd like to do that for you, but would this time perhaps be as good as the other?" Such a reverent spirit honors God.

You can train respectfulness. For example, every so often during your homeschooling stop and have your children repeat after you, "Thank you, Mommy [or Daddy], for instructing me so carefully and for spending your time on me." Sometimes, after studying a specific subject, require that they say "Thank you for math instruction today." After a while it will become so natural to them that they will say it spontaneously. It used to be a requirement in Russia that ballet classes had to end with applause from the students to thank the teacher respectfully.

Accidents

Discern what your children's motives were in discipline situations whenever possible. Motive is everything. Accidents shouldn't be treated like rebellion. Your own knee-jerk responses to all accidents (your own, as well as those of your children) will either show the spirit of Christ or you'll lose an opportunity to teach a message that will register louder than all of your lectures. When you get a flat tire, do you cuss and fume? Or, when you drop and break something, do you clean it up cheerfully and say with your body language, "No big deal?" We sometimes respond to an accident with the words, "Everything works together for good, to those that love the Lord" (Romans 8:28). Parents can recite a verse with the children over the incident and then proceed to clean up the mess. There is no sin in an accident. There is no cause for anyone to register disgust or blame. All of our energies should be directed to *reconstruction* rather than to *criticism*.

Sickness

Now, what of extenuating circumstances? When children are sick, should they be required to be nice, or even obedient? Absolutely! Just because a person gets sick doesn't mean they somehow, now, have a right to be rude. Old people grow either crotchety or sweet, depending upon what their flesh was allowed to get away with when they were young. If mom and dad have to wait until the family schedule isn't chaotic or nobody is sick before they can require godly behavior, powerful lessons of self-denial and endurance will be missed. There will always be an excuse not to train or discipline. Respectfulness and thoughtfulness are always in order.

By the way, it is good not to pay too much attention to scratches and falls, lest you teach children that they get added attention if they are sick or hurt. Hypochondriacs are made in just this way. While holding the injured child, change the subject as quickly as possible onto something productive. Pain is tolerated better while the mind is on something else.

Tell your child, "You're not the first person who's ever has had a sore throat. Teach them to try to suffer quietly. Use sickness to mature your character." (By the way, train your children to sneeze into their elbows and not into their hands. Fewer germs are spread on doorknobs this way.) Require that your children are self-controlled and kind while sick, and THEN you can be compassionate. Don't pamper a cranky spirit in a child.

A note in passing: sudden degradation of behavior (especially if it follows extensive use of antibiotics to treat infections) may be caused by poor ecology in the gut, which is where neurotransmitters are generated. In her CD album, *The Biology of Behavior*, Dianne Craft reports on scientific research that has found a link between the brain, the intestinal tract, and the immune system. Sometimes children act badly because they're physically feeling bad. She reports that three remedies have proved helpful in reversing this trouble: live acidophilus, grapefruit seed extract, and omega 3 oils.[2]

Sibling rivalry

It is all well and good to apply these principles to our children individually, but what of those times when they all get

---

[2] For more information, see http://www.diannecraft.org/

tangled up with one another? A good place to start is to get some **Scripture verses** under their belts, in quiet moments, to draw upon later, in the crossfire of sibling tensions.

"Take heed, lest you eat and devour one another" (Galatians 5:15).

"Be kind and compassionate to one another, forgiving each other, just as in Christ God forgave you" (Ephesians 4:32).

"Bear with each other and forgive whatever grievances you may have against one another. Forgive as the Lord forgave you" (Colossians 3:13).

"Do not repay evil for evil" (1 Peter 3:9).

Secondly, **inspiration** plays a vital role in diminishing sibling conflict. Refer often to the eternal value of each sibling to the other. "Remember that you are going to live with your brother [sister] in heaven forever. Remember that you are going to judge angels together. Remember that God made your brother [sister] for a high purpose." Build up the worth of each other in each other's eyes. Build in respect by having all of the siblings rally behind the achievements and doings of each other. Teach them to show genuine interest in their siblings.

In Scripture it also says, "Behold how good and pleasant it is when brothers dwell together in unity! It is like precious oil poured on the head, coming down upon the beard" (Psalm 133:1-2). The oil of forgiveness is the key to dwelling in unity.

One time when I was a private school teacher I was invited to an unusual home for lunch after church. It was a large extended family with a grandma, and a grandpa living in the home, too. In this home, the grandma made the majority of the meals and the mom was free to have all the babies and homeschool them while they were young. The children were exceptionally well behaved. They were the talk of the whole Christian school. In all respects, it was an exemplary family.

During the meals that I shared with them in their home I noticed that the mother often quietly whispered commands to the children while we ate—and did it so quietly that I hardly realized there was some subtle training going on. When I did realize it, I began to watch her. I saw her go over to one of the children and say, "Would you lean back a bit? You're blocking Susie's view of our guest." Can you imagine training your children to be sensitive to the view-line of others.

This mother had a full-scale course in graciousness going on all the time. Once I gave one of her children a little purse. The mom bent down, prompting her child to say thank you and then continued to provide additional comments for her to say, such as, "I really like all the pockets in it, and the color." The mother whispered to her daughter, "Tell the teacher how thoughtful she was to think of you." She gave her child language for how to be grateful. That mother knew that you don't learn these things in a vacuum.

Once, while we were eating, the older children disappeared out to the front yard with the father—and proceeded to wash my car. Amazing. These children were well trained in sibling teamwork, to the service of others. What you expect out of your children is what you'll get.

That father later told me, "The reason people don't have more children is because they don't discipline them. They hate what their children become. If you love your children you discipline them and you want to have more and more of them. You're curious just to see how different their little personalities will be."

Stick figure eye-openers

A beautiful tool to diffuse sibling rivalry (and for many other training opportunities) is to draw stick figures of a recurring troublesome dynamic between them on a piece of paper so that they can see it objectively. (Always have a stack of scratch paper available for this purpose in your living area. Or use a spiral notebook if you want to save these discussions.)

Nathan the prophet artfully made King David acknowledge his sin by seeing it clearly on someone else first. By the time David heard "thou art the man", his face was on the floor in seconds—no more convincing or explaining was needed.

So, too, we can help our children see the cause and effect of their own behaviors in the issue at hand more clearly by this concrete and visual method. This is one of the best discipline strategies you'll ever hear. It works wonders.

For clarity's sake, use an entire sheet for each concept. If three issues are involved simultaneously, use three sheets of paper. Draw your figures large, loose and fast. Sketch the scenario in the heat of battle, at a moment's notice.

Here are some simple examples of how to draw stick figures to train behaviors in children:

Number One: "You are hitting Susie because she is using nasty words towards you." Draw arrows between figures to show that happening. "The next time she uses nasty words {draw an arrow from one stick figure to the other}, don't you return evil for evil. Instead, you come tell Papa {draw an arrow pointing off the page in the direction of Papa}. Papa will bring pressure to bear upon Susie {draw another arrow pointing down on Susie's head}," etc. Just seeing the trouble on paper helps them to gain a better grip on their behavior with one another.

Number Two: When Ted races in, declaring that Amy kicked him in the backyard, you quickly grab your paper and say, "Well, let's sit down and look at this awful thing together." You sit closely on the couch together, and you begin to quickly draw for him. Sketch two figures, one whose foot is raised, contacting the shin of the other figure. Then you say, "Now what do you suppose caused that little guy's foot to go up like that? Do you suppose something came out of the mouth of the first guy, to cause the foot of the second guy to come up so rudely like that? Draw an arrow from the mouth of Ted to the head of Amy. Then swirl a big circle between both figures and show that one behavior causes another behavior. And your little guy will quietly say: "Oh." End of issue. He'll happily run back outside.

Number Three: Sketch a large water barrel filled halfway with water. (No issue yet, but you want to avoid an issue with this one.) Say: "This is Mommy. Normally, Mommy has lots of things to do {briskly shade in the half-filled barrel with the side of your pencil}, but still has room in the barrel for Susie to talk with Mommy about anything.   But right now, we have company coming in 20 minutes and Mommy's barrel is totally full. {Sketch little waves on top of the barrel and shade in the entire barrel.} If you try to talk with Mommy or need something from Mommy, you'll bump my barrel and I'll slosh all over you. Stay away from Mommy for the next few minutes!!!"

Number Four: "Helen has a ring of personal space around her. {Sketch a happy face, with a three-inch circle around her.} If you grab Helen's book, you've pierced her circle, her personal space. You have to stay outside of her circle, her own private personal space, and ask nicely." (Then erase a little hole in the circle through which Helen passes the book.)

Number Five: Sketch stick figures of 10 people at the dinner table, but only Freddie is constantly talking. Sketch Fred's big mouth wide open with stars coming out of his mouth, surrounding his entire body. Then proceed to sketch frowns on all the other faces all around the table.

Using stick figure drawings can work wonders. Use them!

The quality of your discipline

The best method for ascertaining the quality of your own demeanor while disciplining your children is to ask yourself the simple question, "Would I want to have *me* for a mother, right *now*?" That question will expose to your own heart whether you are fair and loving. Do you discipline out of retaliation and being inconvenienced, or out of genuine love and concern for the development of your child for THEIR sake? So, say it again; say it often: "Would I want to have *me* for a mother?"

Are many of your discipline challenges a result of your own preoccupation? Are you ignoring your kids too frequently, in favor of the phone? Did they draw all over themselves with permanent ink markers because you were not wise in where you left the markers, or your children? Do you leave them alone for too long at a time? Do you take prudent measures to prevent discipline problems before they erupt?

Frequently ask yourself, "Do I want this memory in my child's memory bank?" There is never a second chance to make memories. As we've mentioned before, your child will always remember his childhood through *his* perceptions (regardless of what the reality was), just as you remember yours. What you think of the way your parents raised you is set in concrete. Try to look at what now happens in the home *you* parent. What does your child see through their eyes? Often remind yourself of his vantage point.

If obedience is difficult to come by in your home, look at your own obedience to your husband. Are your responses to your husband full of contention and disrespect? Or, do you respond cheerfully and quickly to his wishes? Is your husband truly the head? If *you* are running the show, you may win the battle now but you may lose your children's hearts in adolescence, if you have not demonstrated a sweet submissive spirit to your husband.

Always keep in mind that **detached discipline** is what you're after. Matching your emotion with your children's emotions is destructive and exhausting. Emotional duking it out will only wear you out. You will escalate in what you say, going on and on about how bad your child is to his face. Getting hooked on the emotional level can result in verbally abusing your child. Instead, command something, and if it is not obeyed immediately and cheerfully, follow it up with some consequence. That way, you'll avoid almost all ruinous verbal combat with your children.

Inconvenient vigilance

The price of achieving Olympic gold medals is **vigilance**. That means exercising **discipline** only over his every hour for ten-plus years, with no let-up, because if he sloughs off for even an hour or two, it will show in the end. Then he might sadly find that if he was sloppy or careless for too many days in that pursuit, he's not going to get the gold. So, too, the price for turning my cantankerous child into a magnanimous adult is responding vigilantly to every attempted defiance.

If you don't like the behavior your child is presently displaying today, you won't like it any *better* tomorrow. If this behavior won't look good on a 16-year-old, don't allow it now. Good parenting requires truckloads of **inconvenient vigilance** and maintaining grit in your resolve. Simply outwit, out-maneuver, out-smart, out-"stubborn" your child every time when it comes to defiant behavior of any kind. If you coddle your child through a fit now, you may find yourself *still* coddling him when he is 35 years old. We've all seen it happen.

You achieve this by making your child's every excursion into defiance very, very costly, not to you, but to him/her. You can do this because in the beginning, for a few short years, God has given you total control over every scrap of food, clothing and shelter your child needs, as well as how your child will spend every minute of every day. The implication of this is that these are the tools to get the job done. You hold all the cards.

When your child is having a fit, pull rank. Live above it. Calmly and strategically make life miserable for **him**, in some little way, as a **direct result**. Show him that it *never* works to **his** advantage. Go at this training relentlessly, like a horse trainer who is putting a stubborn animal through the paces yet again, of cause and effect, cause and effect. Get this message, that "He'll never win if he is defiant", through his little brain, into his spirit, into his gizzard, in every way that you can.

This is the time to have your child repeat the phrase, "Obedience brings blessing; disobedience brings trouble!" in and around and through every head-knocker you have with him. Have him repeat this over and over and over again, day in and day out. Stay at it, ensuring that your child can not only say the phrase, but live the phrase. (Sometimes in quiet moments, you can even start the phrase and have your child finish it: "Obedience brings ___?") Then proceed to show him how true it is in his little life. Help him get the concept, intellectually *and* viscerally. As he grows you can also show him how true it is in other people's lives.

You only have to do this for years and years! You will think they just don't "get it." But then one day, with every child, way past when you think it *should* have happened—poof, you'll notice that for days now you haven't had one head-knocker over *anything*. The defiance just silently goes away. This is the formula: "begin with the law, and then you can relax into grace." Many, many parents begin with grace and have to lay down the law in high school when drugs and knives appear.

You must thoroughly understand that your very young child's fit/tantrum/sullen foot-dragging is not the result of a long "experience-base" with life, or of a seasoned reason. He has no idea what is good for him. It springs from one driving compulsion: self-indulgence. So, in the middle of the scene/crisis don't think it is really something else, "Oh, he doesn't feel well this time/he had a hard sleepless night. If I pacify him just this once by giving in, then it'll all be better."

 Nada. Remember from whence it comes and stand like a brick wall. It is no gift to your *child* to let the child win. It may calm down the moment, smooth things over, and look better in public, but all you did was bury the problem. Stay unflinchingly firm. You can always be wonderfully soft and tender for all the other aspects of the day. It takes both a wise judicious firmness every time it is needed and an habitual loving softness to reflect the true nature of God whom your child will ultimately come to **love to obey** over a lifetime, through this strong, consistent childhood apprenticeship under you!!!

Help from the Holy Spirit

Sometimes you just plain have impasses with your children. At these times, cry out to God for wisdom for what to do. As a schoolteacher, sometimes I would run out of options with really tough kids. I'd go out in the hall and face the wall to pray and softly pound my fist on the wall and say, "Vindicate me, Lord! I've done everything that I know to do." And He would. I'd go back into the classroom and God would make the situation yield. When you reach your own impasse, cry out to God and He will help you with your discipline.

People say, "Oh, I can't hear God; I'm no mystic." That is not true. Scripture says, "My sheep hear my voice" (John 10:3-5, 14-16, 27-28). It is a promise. If you receive an idea while you are praying that you didn't have before, and it's a redemptive idea, believe that it is from God and act upon it. That's the way God works. That is the way God speaks to you.

Just as a farmer has to both plant and pray, so, too does a parent. You parent as if it all depends on you, and then pray as if it all depends on God. Sometimes the need for discipline of your child is unlike any textbook case and nothing seems to work. For these times you need something fresh from the Holy Spirit. Let me give you three "out of the box" examples.

The first has to do with my own daughter and a box of Cheerios®. When she was somewhere around the age of three, she spilled a box of Cheerios® on the floor. I insisted she pick them up. Then I placed her hand on top of them and lifted her hand to the bowl. All she would do was stew and cry. This went on for about 45 minutes, until I was absolutely exasperated. I knew that I had to win, because in winning this one I would secure her obedience for future times. But we were at an impasse. So finally, I left the kitchen, went to my bedroom, fell on my knees, and began to pray. Soon I heard little footsteps, then the hand upon the latch, and then the door open. "Mommy," my daughter said, "Whatcha doin'?" I said, "I'm praying that God will help you obey so that you will grow up to be a straight tree instead of a crooked one, able to please God, too. Do you wanta' come pray with me?" "Yes," she said. And then she planted her pudgy little body down next to mine and we prayed. After prayer we went back to the kitchen and picked up the Cheerios® together. This time her resistant spirit was totally gone.

A second example of gaining help from the Holy Spirit is about an intelligent daughter of a well known Christian speaker who brought home an F on her high school report card. This father flashed a quick "Help" to the LORD. The LORD instantly released him to try something rash. He jumped up, clicked his heels and said, "Well, let's go get some ice cream to celebrate that you finally got that out of your system." The adolescent was totally amazed. She improved her grades, on her own, during the next quarter.

The third instance of supernatural unexpected direction in a discipline case happened at a Christian high school. A high school student with a bad attitude had been truant repeatedly, running away in the middle of the day, which set up a time-consuming chain of events. It occupied several people looking for him and numerous interchanges between parents, teachers and administrators until finally in exasperation one day the headmaster hauled the student into his office and said, "Look, if you were the headmaster in charge of a student such as yourself, what would you do with him?" The student grumbled, "I guess I'd give him a whippin'." The headmaster said "Well, that is highly unusual—to have to do that with a high school student—but if that's all you can come up with, you leave me no choice but to do it, if you run away again. Is that clear?" "Yes," said the boy.

Well, shortly after, true to form, the student ran away again. This time the coach caught the student by the scruff of the neck (the student was smaller than the coach by quite a bit) down the street and marched him back to the school to present him to the head-master. Discouraged, the headmaster said, "What did we arrange in here last time? Refresh my memory. What was it that was going to happen to you if you did this again?" "I'd get a whippin'," came the answer. Suddenly the coach interrupted and addressed the headmaster. "Excuse me, sir; may I speak with you outside for a moment?" Leaving the boy alone, outside, the coach looked intently at the headmaster, took a deep breath, and said, "I'd like to take the whipping for that boy." In the quiet of the moment, it slowly dawning on the headmaster what the coach was doing, he said, "Are you sure?" The coach replied, "I'm sure." They went back into the office. The headmaster eyed the student and said, "Your coach has just offered to take your whipping in place of you. I have agreed that that would settle your offense, so you may now watch." The coach then leaned over the headmaster's desk and the headmaster delivered three strong wincing wallops upon the coach's seat. The coach then walked out of the room.

The headmaster turned to the student and said, "You are free to go now." The stunned student sat riveted in his chair. His headmaster looked up and said "You know, that is just what Christ has done for you, for all your sins. You are free now." It brought the student to his knees and the headmaster then led him to the LORD. Now no one could have initiated that. It wouldn't have worked if the head-master had sought to pre-arrange such a drama; it had to come from the coach. It had to come from the LORD.

These examples show that we may draw upon the LORD far more than we realize for creative, divinely powerful solutions to our discipline challenges. The enemy always wants to convince us that there is no way out. But God always provides a way for us when we seek Him.

Work ethic

And finally, give your children a vision for the work ethic. Perhaps take them to a college dorm and walk them rapidly down the hall. Just slow enough to let them peer into the open rooms to see the utter chaos in the rooms of students who never learned to work. A good model of education is one part academics, one part service (for which the student is paid nothing) and one part work for hire. How many college students do you know who spend any time serving anybody? Too often, we're training overstuffed heads that can't take a minute off to serve anyone. Their dorm rooms show it.

For a second example, take your children to a run-down neighborhood. Teach them that poverty doesn't have to mean filth. Teach them to roll up their sleeves and attack a project and see it through, and actually like doing it, and sing while they work. Surround them with gutsy language about work like "Roman roads weren't built by sitting on the couch all day." "Olympic athletes aren't made out of cream puffs."

Often, the problem with training children to do chores is that parents don't stick with the beginning stages of that training long enough. In the working world, someone who is learning how to detail cars may be required to do 25 cars under supervision before he is turned loose to do one on his own. Someone who is running the cash register at a fast-food restaurant no doubt had to prove himself by serving customers under a watchful eye before he was considered capable of managing the front counter by himself.

So it should be with our own child training. We need to stick with our children longer. Kids hate to do chores, because we abandon them too soon. Employ the "with-you" principle: "Let's tackle this six-foot area together." While you mop the floor, be excited about how dirty your water is becoming. Be enthusiastic about the work and its results. This way, your children catch your emotions about work.

Your work ethic will be caught, not taught. Try to do chores or projects *with* your children for more repetitions than you are accustomed to—and stick with them. Teach them exactly how. Say, "The trash is to be emptied like *this!*" You can teach them to hustle to blast through cleaning the entire house in 20 minutes or less. That way, when they become adults they'll know how.

By the way, when taking those field trips to college dorm rooms and the poor side of town, don't forget to include an old people's home. Point out smiling cheerful examples of the elderly and then point out the grumpy, complaining elderly. Impress upon your children that what they will be like as old persons has a lot to do with the attitudes they form as habits while they are young. You don't just wake up one day thoroughly charming. You work at it, every day, all of your life.

Results

In the end, our aim is that our children will internalize all of our efforts at external discipline, and that they will continue to be self-disciplined in all of their behaviors, even when we are not there—as this last beautiful true story depicts.

A national spelling bee was broadcast in which the final two high school contestants spelled a word that had an "i" in the last syllable. Thousands of dollars were at stake. But in the final minutes the judges and audience were in an uproar of confusion. The first student spelled it correctly; the second student spelled it, but due to the noise in the crowd, no one knew if the student had said an "e" or an "i". The audience was yelling both letters in conflicting favor of their pet contestants. Finally someone said, "Well, let's just ask the student himself. He ought to know which letter he said." A hush fell over the audience. They passed the microphone to the student. "I said the letter `e'—it was the wrong letter." Then as it dawned on the crowd that they had just witnessed a student choosing the truth, and, by the truth, losing the first prize money, they exploded in a standing ovation for that student—and there was not a dry eye in the place. I submit to you that somewhere in that audience there was a set of overcome parents who, years ago, had begun with the end in view.

Part 3:

12 Ways to Trigger the Brain

—with any subject matter!

Here in this section you'll be introduced to another belt of "carpenter's" (educational) tools, to use this time with academics, rather than for training behavior. The contents of this chapter could be called a list of teachers' se-

crets—ones that are never taught in college courses on education. Most beginning teachers do not possess them. They are learned around the campfire of experience, working with hundreds and hundreds of children under a variety of conditions and circumstances. They are what teachers WISH they had learned in college but never did.

This writer has taught nearly every grade level from kindergarten through twelfth, was head of an English department, designed programs for gifted and talented students, and for a year was an elementary school principal. Somewhere along the line I received the teacher of the year award in one of those schools. All this is to say, I loved teaching so much that I gave even my weekends and vacations to the pursuit of a faster and easier way to learn subject after subject.

Over those years I began to see clearly what worked and what didn't work when trying to master new information. Some methods never worked, but some methods worked efficiently all the time—and it is those winning techniques that I'll share with you now.

If you've ever wanted a degree in education, you can forget it. You can relax. If you think you can't do a good job without a degree in education, you're mistaken, you can. Gaining these tools will save you somewhere between $40,000 and $120,000 (for four years of college) trying to get a degree where you won't learn these things. But what you'll save in money is nothing compared to what you will save in hassle, head-knockers, no-takes and stress within your family as you try to teach and be a parent.

In the same way that an experienced carpenter puts on a belt of the finest tools that he has before tackling any job, so you as a parent can benefit from having an array of sharp tools to help you educate your young ones. Keep in mind that these are only ready tools for you to draw from when you need them. You won't use all of them all of the time. You may feel a bit like you're drinking from a fire hydrant to hear about them all at once, but when you've finished learning about them, you will discover that you are able to use them with skill at precisely the right moments.

Before discussing each of these tools, let's begin with a simple overview of what to teach, and why. Since the universe was created with intelligent design, we can divide what we study into two grand parts. We study the words of God and the works of God. The words are the Bible; His works are what He has made. We study both areas because they each shed light and insight upon the other. For a discussion of how to learn what's in the Bible, see our homeschool how-to #56, *How to Cultivate a Lasting Love of the Bible in Your Children*.  Presently, we'll focus upon strategies for studying all of the other disciplines: biology, anatomy, geography, etc.—all of which comprise His **works**.

To start, let's define **optimal teaching** or **optimal learning**. It is the process of gaining the greatest amount of growth, in the shortest amount of time, as effortlessly as possible.

Why *the greatest amount of growth*? Because the more we know and the more skills we conquer, the broader a person we become. That means the more we can serve our fellow man. Why develop only half of our capacity? If each evening, each week, each month is used wisely, we can become extraordinary people. I knew a missionary who visited his dentist while he was home on furlough and learned how to pull teeth. He learned this skill in one afternoon, and when he went back to Africa he ended up pulling scores of teeth over the rest of his years there, delivering scores of people from untold suffering.

Why *in the shortest amount of time*? Because there is so much to learn. We are in an age of an information explosion. What there is to know is increasing geometrically, compounding. One simply cannot keep up with it. There is no time to read anything twice—with the exception of the Bible, which, of course, should be read over and over, for retaining wisdom in the midst of such a boom of facts and figures and inventions and discoveries and opinions and experiments!

And why *as effortlessly as possible*? If it is possible to gain knowledge by an easier route, then we should take that route. This diffuses emotional resistance and mental fatigue for the learner. Why ram your truck up against the front gate of an estate when there is a driveway around back, in the alley, where the servants' quarters are? Back there, there is no gate, and the servants zip in and out with no problem.

We're going to identify more than a dozen tools that will be like little cars that transport us up these easy driveways into the brain. But first, we have one more division to make. Under the broad category of studying the **works** of God we're going to further divide what it is that we will study into two more large categories. They are **academics** and **skills**. They are each taught and learned very differently from the other. Over the course of a lifetime we want to acquire a fair knowledge of a broad spectrum of academics and we also want to acquire skills in all sorts of areas. Such skills might include, for example athletics, music, domestic tasks, car mechanics, house construction, etc.

The optimal way to learn *academics* is by narration. The optimal way to learn *skills* is by:

(1.) splintering each skill into small pieces,
(2.) learning each small piece in short spurts, and
(3.) reinforcing it with spaced repetition.

~~~~~~~~~~~~~~~~~~~~~~~~~~

Now let's take a closer look at each tool on our educational belt. We'll begin with **teaching academics**.

1. NARRATION: BEING ABLE TO FIRE BACK INFORMATION

You teach academics by having your child interact with those academics. If information simply lies on a page, you can bet "nobody is home!" "The elevator isn't going all the way to the top floor."

A student must *do* something with what he reads in order to make it his own. An apple on a plate does nothing for you, until you eat it. It is the same with information. It must be processed somehow.

The act of summarizing *is* that process by which a child begins to understand and retain information. Summaries can be made in three ways: by speaking, writing, and drawing. Later, when the child is of high school age he will engage in the advanced speaking that is called rhetoric. Rhetoric is the art of becoming persuasive with your summarized information.   For starters, however, your child can fire back summaries to you in one of the easier first three ways.

The summarization process is far superior to taking a multiple choice test, where someone else processes information and limits you to picking from those pre-determined options. When a person has to summarize, he necessarily and subconsciously bonds with the part of the material which is most valuable to him, intellectually and emotionally. *Why* a child chooses to bond with one part of the information and another child picks an entirely different part, is a matter of God-given wiring. We can imagine that as young children Thomas Edison would always bond with the practical implications of information, Napoleon the political part and Bach the philosophical part.

While summarizing, each of these individuals subconsciously ran through Bloom's taxonomy of higher level thinking skills without being aware of it. Bloom's hierarchy of thinking[3] begins on the simple, concrete level with being able to sequence information, apply it to memory, and look for patterns. It graduates to complex abstractions of thought such as synthesis, evaluation, judgment, and the application of wisdom to the information at hand. In order to re-tell the

---

[3] B. Bloom, B. Mesia, and D. Krathwohl, *Taxonomy of Educational Objectives* (two volumes: *The Affective Domain* & *The Cognitive Domain*) (New York: David McKay, 1964).

information, all of these levels have been rapidly scanned through in the brain, with far more precision than a computer could do it, in order to pick *what* to tell and the *why* of it.

So what does all of this look like, fleshed out? How do you *do* this? When the child is little, start with a short section of information. The younger the child, the shorter the section. Start with just one paragraph so that he will have success. You might pick a section from a simple biography of Alexander the Great, or any number of topics from a young person's easy-to-read encyclopedia set. Tell the child that he is going to have to repeat back to you, in his own words, what it is that you have just read to him. Knowing that he will soon have to speak to you (or draw a simple picture) rivets his attention upon the material at hand, so that there is no broken focus in his concentration. Artfully package what you are doing in a fun, encouraging atmosphere and you'll gain the child's cooperation. Beginnings are important.

When he has conquered being able to paraphrase a paragraph, then build his mental capacity with longer and longer portions as he grows older. Finally, the child will habitually be able to read any text himself, close the book, and immediately write a good summary. From early on, teach him that the more details he can recall, the better. (You may even give him a penny or a raisin for each fact that he can remember, just to prime the pump; we call this "penny narration.") This process quickens the mind. If begun early, this will become "old hat" to the adult, so trained—as natural as digestion. Lifetime reading and reflection are what make for a truly cultured person. A notebook full of notes

on all of one's past reading can become a favored possession.

Excerpts from history and biography make good material
upon which to begin cultivating this intellectual rigor in your
children. After initial training, these oral narration sessions
can be done casually, while taking walks, riding in the car or
cooking dinner, by asking the simple question: "Tell me
about what you are reading—tell me anything and everything." Not too long down the road, you won't be able to
keep your children quiet for the sheer joy of looking forward
to telling you what they've read. If listening to all of these
summaries from a number of children becomes too demanding upon you, a child can audio-record his summaries
all by himself. He'll love hearing himself on replays of the
recording, which will even further cement the material in his
mind. Occasionally, he could even narrate to brothers and
sisters, too.

Remember, this is just a tool, and a very fine one at that. So
if a child is resistant, come at it more subtly, through the
back door. Or if he is learning through a standard curriculum, you could encourage him to talk about a topic from his
studies later at dinner. By carefully using this tool you will
help shape a very articulate child, who is broadly conversant
on a whole range of topics, who grows to think logically and
concisely, and has no fear in expressing himself.

If you use this tool to *hammer* a child, it will backfire. Sometimes a tool should be dropped for a while and picked up
again later when negative emotional factors aren't present.
Think of yourself as a fine surgeon, or sculptor, who knows
his tools well and lays them down and picks them up

sometimes with lightning speed as the moment warrants. Teaching children well takes every bit as much skill, and the results are far more eternal.

2. DRAW SIMPLE PICTURES

A second means of processing information is for a young child to DRAW stick figures of what happened. Drawing stick figures to narrate has the added advantage of lodging the information in the right hemisphere of the brain (the picture side), as well as the left, for stronger recall. When a child takes words and reassimilates them into pictures he has triggered both sides of his brain.

In the beginning, a child will only be able to speak the summary or draw these stick figures. But after the skill of writing itself is mastered, the child will be involved more and more in writing the summary. Therefore, begin that writing process at about the third grade, or so. Simple summary sentences can be attempted earlier.

> **In summary,** these first two brain triggers are the ability to summarize information, either by (1) speaking/writing   or   (2) simple drawing.

Now let's move on to the task of teaching **skills.** As we mentioned before, it will take three triggers to conquer this very different kind of learning. But first of all, let's define a skill. It is any activity that you repeat over and over with greater and greater precision and excellence. In Proverbs it says, "See a man skilled in his labor; he will stand before kings." In 1 Kings 7:13-45 we read that King Solomon sought out an artisan by the name of Hiram from a far away region, and hired him to help build the temple. His work was recorded in the Bible, for people of all time to read about, because he was "highly skilled and experienced in all kinds of bronze work." Having good skills can allow you to ride on the heights of the earth, even if a good handle on academics (generalized knowledge) doesn't. Skills can be vitally important. So let's find out the best way to learn skills via triggers 3, 4 and 5.

3. SKILLS: SPLINTERING THE TASK

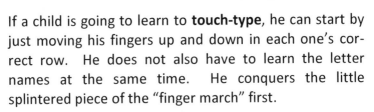

When beginning a new skill, break it down into its tiniest parts. Isolate each part of the skill that has never been done before. Conquer each small piece first and then when you put it all together, it'll be "butter on toast!"

Here are some examples:

If a child is going to learn to **touch-type**, he can start by just moving his fingers up and down in each one's correct row. He does not also have to learn the letter names at the same time. He conquers the little splintered piece of the "finger march" first.

Similarly, if a child begins learning to play the **piano**, he can start with playing chords, without attempting to read music at the same time. Then, he can proceed to learn the various rhythm patterns, using only one note, without reference to either chords or note reading.

When a child is learning to **cook**, he can conquer one small thing at a time. When cracking eggs, for example, crack a full dozen, until he fully gets the hang of it; someone more experienced can then make the eggs into an omelet.

If a child is learning **math** facts, try learning only one set per week. If he encounters problems even at that level, then only tackle two or three individual facts at a time.

Get the principle? *Conquer the small pieces in isolation first.* Then, when your child puts them together, all the brain has to do is jump the synapses between the already acquired mini-skills. The entire new skill will seem easy because you tricked the brain into mastering the small pieces first. At the end, only a little mental effort is needed to finish the job of putting it all together. This is far superior to feeling mentally clobbered and overwhelmed by too much, too fast. Very complex difficult skills can be learned easily in just this manner.

4. SKILLS: SHORT SPURTS
Require the brain to do the new activity in short spurts. When acquiring new material, spurting will outdo suspended time, hands down.

Remember this phrase, "less is more." An overwhelmed, tired, bewildered brain will only shut down on you. Short piano lessons, short tennis lessons, short math lessons is the optimal way to begin. Stop the activity before the child wants to, while the emotions are still running high.

Children learning to play the violin in Japan begin by first just holding the instrument in the correct position, to which the relatives all vigorously applaud in approval. The instrument is put away. The next day, the child steps onto the stage, again with the instrument in the correct position and her posture "picture-perfect." The relatives applaud even more robustly. Again the instrument is put away. And so on and on it goes—all the way to the Juilliard School of Music.

5. Skills: Spaced Repetition

And finally, repeat the material often. Ever had the experience of going to bed at night not being able to figure something out, only to awake in the next morning with the solution? That is because your brain incubates information on the subconscious level, when you're not directly focused upon it, consciously. This is the value of spaced repetition.

Imprint the autonomic nervous system strongly and then get off it. Let some time elapse, then imprint it with the same material again a second time and again a third, spacing your repetitions. By resting in between, your brain will synthesize all new material without alarm, and gain a solid competency within mere days. Our own Zoom-Type and Quick Piano courses[4] were invented and designed using these three triggers, almost exclusively. Because keyboarding skills are so easily learned by this method, students around the world have learned to type in five days instead of taking a year, and have played their first chord overnight, romping up and down the keyboard, sounding like Beethoven to themselves.

~~~~~~~~~~~~~

Now let's move on to a different batch of triggers. These triggers have to do with *when* to learn or teach new information.

6. SCHEDULE ACTIVE VS. PASSIVE PERIODS
This is one of my favorite triggers because it works so extremely well, especially with the young ones. The idea here is to, at first, vigorously work the cerebral thinking part of the brain for a short while, and then switch to work the motor planning or physical part of the brain, alternating back and forth. For very young children you can even alternate active vs. passive minutes, one right after the other. This keeps your children thoroughly awake and alive to both

---

[4] Zoom-Type and Quick Piano, at www.homeschoolhowtos.com.

types of tasks and gets double the productive output during your scheduled academic hours (or all day, for that matter).

You may use either chores or physical exercise for your active sessions. I personally like to use chores because you get the school work done and your house cleaned at the same time. Using a combination of them is terrific.

Developing the habit of daily checking off academics, chores, grooming, athletics and music on to-do charts will lead to hundreds of triumphant checkmarks for your children. Using charts breeds success even on the first day that you use them. For great tips on how to do this exactly, order our booklet/e-book/Kindle book #105 on *How to Make Optimal Homeschooling To-Do Charts.*

Physical exercise is extremely important to a growing child and often has the advantage of helping them to throttle back their tendency to be hyperactive during quiet moments where they need to be attentive. Consider purchasing a mini-trampoline so that they can have access to really good exercise year round, rain or shine. Be sure that it is a high-quality soft bounce, to minimize joint pain and trouble for their future years.[5]

---

[5] Order a Needak® soft-bounce folding rebounder at www.homeschoolhowtos.com for less than the manufacturer's retail price.

Do you see how this works? You have your child do one row of math problems, then have him hop up to make the bed, then back to another row of math, then up to go empty the trash, then another row of math, then out to jog around the outside of the house five times, etc. Or have him read one chapter of history, go pick up just three things to put away in his room; put up three more things after the next chapter, etc. That way, neither the academics nor the chores ever seem overwhelming to the child, and they both get done. The younger the child is, the more benefit he'll receive from alternating these activities.

Remember that this is just a tool. If the child seems wonderfully attentive and happy and awake during his academics, hold off with the "jumping up and down" tool. Sometimes even the barometric pressure outside will affect a child's attention span. When I used to do recess duty in the public schools, the veteran teachers would often remark after observing the children roughly play (or fight), "There must be a storm coming." And sure enough, it would rain that afternoon.

7. TEACH OR LEARN TOUGH SUBJECTS DURING HIGH VOLTAGE TIMES

High voltage times are when the blood sugar is high and the child has had sufficient rest. You're just asking for trouble to try to teach something new when the brain doesn't have enough glucose to fire very fast. For some people, high voltage times are right after meals. For others, that is their

most sluggish time. Some children are nocturnal. It's far easier to teach them something new in the evening. For others, the early morning is their finest hour. You don't need to cater to these patterns all the time. And a person's patterns may change over time. Jill may have had her prime times at 8 in the morning when she was seven, but when she turned 14 her best time for learning was 8 at night. And, a nocturnal person might have to work at a day time job, eventually, in the real world. But knowledge of these patterns in your children can be used to great advantage when you try to teach them anything new. For most children, giving them a healthy snack (no sugar) immediately prior to a mentally challenging session works wonders.

Make sure that you aren't on the bleeding edge of gaining new ground in all of your subjects at once. While carving out new territory in one subject, try to just mark time in all of the other subjects with enriching, reinforcing activities, so that you don't frustrate and exhaust both you and your child.

8. USE SMALL MOMENTS WISELY

Years of mental advantage are lost through missing small learning moments—while standing in grocery store lines, riding in the back of a car, waiting on family members to get into the car, waiting at traffic lights, etc. At the very least, have your children carry life-enhancing, thought-provoking good books with them at all times, and insist that they read them when they are "waiting." Idle time is bad stewardship.

I remember reading in a *Reader's Digest* article years ago that if you devote 15 minutes a day to learning a subject or practicing a skill, you will soon become an expert because the majority of other people will never be that consistent. Be on the lookout for small segments of time in your day that you and your children can use to great advantage to further your own larger written goals or the goals you have for your children. Some home educating parents wait until they have their lives totally in order each morning before beginning work with the children, whereas if they had required their children to use small moments wisely, children could have had several subjects out of the way while they were still in their pajamas.

Dangle the motivation in front of them that if they'll use every second well to conquer their schooling each day, it means more free time for them later on. Then see to it that their "free" time is wholesomely directed toward (1.) developing a home based business of their own that they absolutely love, (2.) reading fabulous classical books that they think they picked out because you offered them a choice from a pre-selected list (download Melanie's excellent book list from our website) or (3.) becoming the world's greatest bassoon player! Challenge, inspire, motivate.

After months of working yourself into a lather with little mini-sermonettes on the value of using every minute, don't be shocked if your children really "get it" and take off in productivity beyond what you now imagine. If your children use every minute wisely, they *could* race ahead of their peers, graduate early, have their own paid-for land and home, etc. When it finally clicks, they may rise at 6 a.m., have their schooling done by 10 a.m., waltz into the kitchen, make six blueberry pies from scratch, sing hymns as they work, and clean up the place, too! You may find yourself sitting in the living room, shaking your head, big tears running down your face. Was this what all that parenting work was for? You might not have dreamed you could see such results. Your children may

Memory Moments 8.

USE TIME WISELY

Susanna Wesley, who home schooled her many children including John and Charles, read a multitude of books whilst cooking meals.

not **stop** being self-disciplined. They may save thousands of dollars from working odd jobs by the time they are 12, launch inventions, and write books. In fact, you may have to pull them *off* of their work sometimes, because they get going so hard. Far better this, than depression, self-absorption, and aimless boredom, so common to adolescents.

As a parent, trying to homeschool (raising children) is a lot like trying to rev up an old dead Model T Ford. You wind and grind the hand lever in a circle in the front of the vehicle over and over, to get it started. Then you rip around behind it and kick it from the rear, and then you run around to the front again and remove all of the big stones in the road, to make it easier for the little jitney to get goin'. When the old Model T actually does start up and putt-putt-putts right off, all by itself, you just stand there in shock—amazed. It actually works! Well, just what did you *think* would happen!?!

Great things are at stake over the loss or gain of small moments.

9. TEACH FOR WHOLE BODY INSTRUCTION

When you want to teach (and/or learn) something new, involve as many of the five senses as you can. Consider ways in which your children can hear, see, touch, taste and smell the concepts. Don't worry about figuring out who is an auditory or visual or kinesthetic learner. Teach to all modalities as often as possible. Can you record a part of it and play it back to them? Can you rhyme the information and have them sing it? Is there a way to picture it? Is there some way that they can touch, manipulate, or rearrange the information? Could you possibly even have them smell it and taste it somehow? That is why travel is such a strong learning environment: it engages all five senses. You eat the cuisine and smell the air. When you get off the plane in Bombay you *smell* India, you *taste* India, you *feel* its heat.

Auditory learning: *What I HEAR, I may grasp.*

Visual learning: *What I SEE, I may remember.*

Kinesthetic learning: *What I DO, I understand.*

The theory here is: what the octopus holds with *eight* legs is held much more strongly than what he holds with *two*. By involving more of the body, a person is able to learn and retain far more information.

10. USE AN ANALOGY OR OBJECT LESSON TO NAIL POINTS

If you are the teacher, drive a concept home by using an analogy or object lesson. If you are the learner, try to figure out how to convert the material you are studying into an object lesson or an analogy. That process will cement the information solidly for quick recall.

Here's an example that you will probably never forget, because the object lesson is so perfect. Let's say that you need to explain to small children how forgiveness works. You want to drive home the concept that they need to forgive frequently in order to navigate through life with emotional freedom and not get bogged down in counterproductive bitterness.

10. Analogy or Object Lesson

Take two peaches and set them on a counter. Pierce each of them with a separate nail. Remove the nail from one, but keep the nail in the other. Explain that "When we are wounded by someone's words or actions, it is like this nail going into a peach. If we don't quickly remove the nail by forgiveness, the wound of bitterness will grow. Let's leave the nail in one peach on the counter for a week. We will soon see it fester and mold all over the counter. But if we remove the nail immediately (now pick up the other peach) we will see that the skin of the peach will close over the hole and we all will forget that the peach was ever pierced. We'll forget that the incident ever happened."

All of us tend to remember children's sermons better than the main sermon because the preacher uses an object to drive his point home.

11. DRIVE A NEW CONCEPT INTO INNER SPEECH

This trigger works like this: first you say the phrase, and then you whisper the phrase, and finally you just think the phrase. If you are trying to learn a dance step, for example, you would *SAY* "slide, together, back" as you are doing the step. Then you would *WHISPER* "slide, together, back" as you repeat the step. And finally you would just *THINK* the phrase as you did the step one more time.

Let's say that you were trying to learn tennis. The first thing you had to learn was to pull your racket back immediately after hitting the ball over the net, in order to get ready to return either a forehand or a backhand volley. So at first you *say* (as you prepare to hit the ball) "racket back". Then you would *whisper* "racket back" as you prepare to hit the ball again. Finally, you would just *think* "racket back" when preparing to hit the ball a third time. Now you have driven the concept into inner speech and you'll do it automatically from here on out. To summarize the essence of this trigger:

> **SAY and do,**
> **WHISPER and do,**
> **THINK and do.**

12. SINK AN EMOTIONAL HOOK IN FIRST, THEN FOLLOW WITH THE FACTS

Knowledge will be stored more effectively if you first get the emotions fired, then tack on as many additional facts as possible before that temporary excitement for learning wanes.

For example, after reading from the Bible about the Exodus, students can study where the Nile River is located, what a scroll is, and what history was being made at that time in Egypt.

12. Follow emotional hooks with facts

For teaching very young people, this means you follow reading children's stories with teaching science, geography or some other relevant subject. Take, for example, their excitement over Humpty Dumpty. At the close of the story while they are still bright-eyed and bushy tailed you can now teach them about gravity, the three parts of an egg, and King's men (England's changing of the guard), for example, or lessons about irreversible failure. (To see just how far you can take this with a gifted child see our how-to's item #53, *Humpty Dumpty Intellectual Stretch*.) Or, read a story about a tin soldier, then follow it with a discussion of metals—tin, copper, brass, etc. After each story, teach until their eyes glaze over and you can tell they've finally shut down. But as long as they are emotionally open after that story, it's prime teaching time.

For high schoolers, you can ignite this emotional trigger by beginning academics with <u>reading biographies</u>. It's so easy to learn science or history once you are emotionally warm toward the people.

Realizing the importance of this principle, it is well worth the effort to occasionally seek out experts or tutors <u>who are passionate about their subject matter</u>—not just taking home a paycheck. The right teacher can bring the most boring topics to life. It is worth traveling far distances to temporarily sit under such people. Mentoring, even for just an afternoon, can have a profound affect upon one's life.

Happy emotions diffuse academic stress. Compelling stories make learning facts and figures far easier.

13. GET ANOTHER ANGLE FOR NO-TAKES

You'll notice when a student is simply not getting it. You'll read it in the body language. The eyes will glaze over; the student will withdraw, protest, cry, and grow stiff. It will manifest itself in such statements as "I couldn't possibly do that math problem, 'cause I just sprained my eyebrow!"

The common (and failing) solution traditionally has been to 1) teach it the same way only louder, or 2) up the dosage ("Then you'll have it for homework!"). The best solution, instead, is to stop doing it and then attack it in a new way later in the same day or on another day. Try a smaller dose.

Figure out how to tie it to something he already knows. In short, change your teaching style. For more help with this order our booklet on *Motivation: Academic Energizer.*

Often, the very best strategy is to move back a level, some-

times all the way back to the concrete level. The concrete level precedes the abstract level in the development of mental ability. Concrete means the level at which you see real things corresponding with abstract concepts. In math, for example, the child begins with one shoe plus one shoe equals two shoes. He later understands that one plus one equals two in *any* setting, and he doesn't need to see the shoes anymore. Eventually, he moves to the ability to think abstractly in every area. Some children advance to this level earlier, some later. You may think you can assume your child has the ability to think abstractly because of his age, but it is the degree of his mental **frustration** that gives you the clue that it may be a relief to him to move back a degree to the concrete level again for awhile, thus building a firmer bridge to the higher more abstract level.

Two examples:

When teaching a young piano student to keep the same hand position to play the same chord up an octave or down an octave, the student's undisciplined hand would habitually go limp. After stressing the concept of keeping the same hand position several times, there was no improvement. So, I left off the command, went and picked up a statue that we had in the house, and had the student feel it. Then I said, "Now YOU stand like a statue, be so firm that I cannot push you over." Success! Then we moved back to the piano and now he held his hand quite stiff in the proper chord position for the new chord up an octave. Moving back to the concrete level solved the problem.

When teaching a young gymnastic student to do cartwheels on a diagonal line on the stage for a performance, the student repeatedly did them only in a horizontal line. Again, after repeating the command several times, there was no understanding. I then went and got a stack of magazines and dropped them one by one on the floor in the intended diagonal line. Immediately, the student did the cartwheels alongside the magazines, correctly. Again, moving back to the concrete level solved the problem.

When you begin to see that teaching any concept to your child is a "no-take"—judging from his degenerating attitude—stop. (Have the child do one more problem or read one more paragraph so that he doesn't think that his bad attitude won him the privilege of quitting; *then* you be the one to drop it.) After that, try touching on the hated subject just *barely* each day. Make a baby step of progress and then get off it. Soon, you'll be able to pick up speed again, because you've diffused the emotional struggle by not requiring much and the child's brain has had some small successes. For more on this, order our *Teaching the Resistant Student*: eight reasons for resistance.

~~~~~~~~~~~~~~~~~~~~~~~

There now, that completes the first 13 ways to trigger the brain. What follows is a list of further ways that you can trigger the brain. They are not as important as the first dozen+ ways, but nevertheless, knowing about them can further ease your way. They are additional effective tools.

14. USE PLACEMAT GROUNDING
Have four placemats within grabbing distance of your favorite chair: (1) a world map, (2) a U.S. map, (3) a diagram of outer space and all the planets, and (4) a timeline (you may have to make that one—maybe attach it to the back of one

of the other placemats). Refer to these four placemats all the time as you prepare for stories, history, news events, etc. Ground all new information to the big picture all the time.

14. Use placemats

15. TRAIN KEEN OBSERVATION THROUGH DRAWING

Those who make great contributions to mankind are those who have paid attention to detail in some way. Most geniuses exhibit keen observation skills. They grasp detail that the ordinary man passes by. They use the input of detail to then come to new and larger general conclusions.

The best way to train keen observation is by cultivating the skill of sketching—even in very young children. Use coloring books only for *tracing*, so children learn how to bend lines to create images. The common practice of coloring IN the pictures does absolutely nothing to develop the child's mind. Have children draw the actual object, tracing right over the lines of the coloring book picture, either slightly inside or slightly outside the lines that are already there.

Most elementary art courses do very little to sharpen visual acumen, either. These elementary classes often are aimlessly absorbed with having children manipulate a great variety of stuff like sequins, feathers, clay, etc. Conversely, daily contributing to a sketch book with increasingly complex line drawings will mature the growing mind wonderfully.

Have very young children begin by tracing hundreds of simple coloring book pictures. (Avoid buying complex pictures. One clear image per page is what you look for in a good coloring book.) The next step (as is explained in more detail in our homeschool how-to #54: *Teach Your Children to Draw*) is to fold these same pictures in half, then tape them to paper and have the children draw the other half of the picture. This does wonders to teach proportion. They can then flip the picture to the other half and draw the other side. Then remove the picture entirely and the child will have his/her own complete drawing on the paper. For the third step in drawing, simply stand the same picture up before the child and have him draw the full picture only by looking at it.

After drawing simple pictures becomes easy, continue by looking at paintings by the masters while trying to imitate what they have done. Norman Rockwell's black and white sketches are superb to use because children are taken with the subject matter of these pictures, and the lines can somewhat be mastered, at least in a crude way. Continue on with Rembrandts, etc. Keep students learning composition and line from these masters. Development of an understanding of color, tint and shade can come much later.

16. Don't delegate too soon

Most people have horrendous problems with delegation — even in the business world. The problem is that they delegate too soon and check up on it too infrequently. A task should not be delegated until it has been done numerous times to perfection, in your presence, without you saying a word. Because it has been done once right doesn't mean it will be repeated in the same manner the minute you turn your back. It must be consistently done multiple times in your presence, before a "trainee" can be depended upon to do it right, when alone. This is particularly true of chores.

When teaching your children how to empty the trash throughout the house, for example, training is not complete until they know: 1) the order in which to empty the waste baskets, 2) how to insert new bags into each basket, 3) how to refrain from going through the trash and retrieving lost treasures, 4) how to deposit the trash outside in the large can, and 5) how to do it in record time without dilly-dallying. The point is that this task is not trained until the child has perhaps done it without comment from you the correct way 25 times, while still in **your presence**. *Then* you can delegate. But even then see to it that you come back two days later and double check, then a week later.

This principle is especially true with the training of penmanship—both printing and cursive. Most teachers take their eye off the process far too soon and then groan that the child has slipped into bad habits  when they weren't looking. Never let the child form the letters wrong for the first several weeks and the brain will make a lifetime habit of making the correct stroke. Delegate too soon and writing will become an endless hassle. The key point about this trigger is that **internal discipline** is slowly acquired by having many experiences of **external discipline** under the watchful eye of an attentive teacher.

17. TRAIN CRITICAL THINKING SKILLS

"Do you walk to work or take your lunch?" is not a logical statement. The second phrase doesn't proceed from the first. It is a logical fallacy. Scores of far more subtle remarks are totally missed by the average high school students of today, making them sitting ducks for manipulation by advertisers and cults. Using our homeschool how-to title #6, *Critical Thinking Skills*, you'll be able to train them right out of this mental fog into crystal-clear tight thinking. They'll first learn to distinguish fact vs. opinion, then move on into advertising strategies, followed by a whole battery of logical fallacies for which they will learn their Latin names and definitions. They'll also learn to distinguish one fallacy from another. This critical thinking packet is loaded with funny examples of mixed-up thinking, making it very easy to learn.

18. BUSY CHILDREN ARE HAPPY CHILDREN

Here we see this concept repeated. This concept is basic not only to optimize behavior, as we've previously discussed under the training section of this book but also for academics. Stay ahead of your children with enough activities and challenges. Too much idle time multiples discipline challenges and academic sloth. If you have adolescents, make sure that they are absolutely swimming in too much to do. This diminishes the time that is available for too much introspection, depression, and aimlessness while their hormones are banking off the walls. Give them compelling goals. (See our title #48, *How Not to Waste Your Youth*.)

19. NO NEED FOR GRADING

The public system of education is big on labeling. Of what value are grades in the elementary years? Isn't it quite like trying to grade a tulip? Whatever is it for? Why would an oak tree need a grade? Instead, plan curriculum for good continuous growth. Growing is all that matters.

20. TEACH FOR MASTERY INSTEAD OF PLOWING THROUGH CURRICULUM

In the tutorial system of home education you can stay on a page until it is thoroughly understood, or you can re-teach a concept again and again until it is mastered. Contrast that to the public school system of merely plowing through curriculum, where the top students are bored and the slower ones are in over their heads. The *book* gets "covered" by the end of the year, but what about the *student*?

21. GO WIDE WHEN YOU CAN'T GO FORWARD

If you can see that your child is beginning to get in over his head academically, go back to a previous level. Enrich and stabilize. Strengthen the foundation with further examples. Begin to build again, later, only when the fear is diffused.

22. USE A MOTIVATIONAL PRIZE BOX

Reserve any small thing that you would normally just *give* your children; make them *earn* it by doing some tough piece of academics. Hardly ever just *give* a child *anything*. Get academic mileage out of the least little thing. For example, tell the child, "You can have something from the prize box if you will do all your scales again on the piano," or "You can have a prize if you do one line of math problems." This works great for whatever they doggedly just don't want to do, whatever feels like pulling teeth, whatever seems formidable. Just break these albatrosses into lots of small tasks to just get some movement going in that direction, and offer a prize. To avoid materialism, check out our homeschool how-to #25, *Goofy Little Rewards for Children*. Many of these clever rewards are not *things* and don't cost money. They are unusual prizes that can provide a little spur, a little motivation, to help a child over a rough patch of academics or an overwhelming chore.

23. TEACH YEAR 'ROUND

Everyone has different opinions about this one, but it has been my experience that this diffuses panic and stress. If

you teach year around, you can go slower and yet always be ahead. It seems that this is more natural and fits in with the varying seasons of family life. If you have company for two weeks in the winter when the children can receive valuable social training and augmented creative play, then why crowd it with academics? Proceed with the academics when the other kinds of excitements are lower and when academics are a blessing to keep ordinary days full of challenge, progress and luster. The family will never have a boring day with this approach. Teaching year 'round also eliminates the need for review.

24. Tight, rigorous moral training but low-stress nourishing academic education

Placing children in high-, middle- and low-ability reading groups labels them right away. In public schools this is the beginning of stressful comparative academic training. At the same time, many opportunities for disciplining sour attitudes are missed or ignored altogether in the public school arena. In both cases, we should strive to do exactly the opposite. If your child lies, land on him like there's no tomorrow. But if he is having difficulty learning to read, diffuse his stress, take time to be careful, do it thoroughly and major on encouragement.

25. Do re-runs for discipline and attitude training

If children enter or exit a room with a surly attitude, call them back to the point in the room where they made their entrance and make them "re-run that scene" with the proper attitude. Make them return to the place in the yard where they had a fit and re-run the proper response, etc. As we have previously noted, the geographic positioning of them to re-run the event is excellent for grounding the good habit in the autonomic nervous system.

26. Talk your way through the encyclopedia

This gives you an endless avenue of communication around _ideas_—rather than focusing on _people_ (which tends toward gossip) or _things_ (which tends to lead into materialism). Encyclopedic knowledge provides for marvelous non-stressful ongoing stimulation. Reading through an old thrift store **children's** set of The Golden Book Encyclopedia will fill your children's heads with scores of interesting facts. Because the set is loaded with pictures, it makes for continuous fun mental activity at no extra work to you. Just 15 minutes of this reading a day will broaden their minds immeasurably. Remember to have them narrate back to you about what they've just read, if you want them to retain any info.

27. STRIVE FOR A QUIET, PRODUCTIVE MIND, LEARNING IN AN ENVIRONMENT WHERE THERE IS NOT ALWAYS SOMETHING BLARING INTO IT

Two or three quiet reading hours in the evening over the course of 10 years yields staggering results. Playing the radio and background music (not to mention TV/DVD's) often robs the mind of heightened focused productive thinking. For some food for thought in that area you may want to read our title #34 on *TV Watching out of Control: Hidden Problems for Adults and Children*.

The longer you can keep your children away from the media, the more they will read. No exposure to media until fourth grade will make lifetime voracious readers of them, because only through reading will they get to move outside of their practical daily life and broaden their horizons. They will run to this wholesome place repeatedly. Media provides stimulation, but stimulation often is a far cry from intellectual growth.

28. AVOID COMPARING AND COMPETING

Avoid allowing yourself or your children to waste excessive curiosity on the lives of **celebrities**—politicians, musicians, movie stars, or anyone else. Recognize any addiction to magazines and any YouTube, Face book and Twitter online idolatry, and cut it off. Idol worship is a consummate waste, destroying endless productive hours, often starting with the junior high and senior high years. The more concentration we give to celebrities, the less time is available for us to improve our own lives.

Avoid <u>competition</u>, too. Again, whatever is it for? Why pit piano students one against another, merely to give a prize for the top proficiency? Why not rather have each student go and serve with his music (at whatever level he has attained) at an old people's home or day care center? This way your children give back to God their skills, rather than puffing themselves up with pride. There are plenty of ways to motivate students without resorting to the pressure of having to be better than others.

29. AVOID USING A COMPUTER IN THE EARLY YEARS
(until about the 4th grade)

We've just talked about TV and video; likewise, too much stimulation from the computer screen makes the child a responder instead of a producer. There will be a lifetime to be computer driven—where it will be a "have-to". Why rob the early years? The visual fixation it requires overloads the nervous system and narrows the field of life far too soon. It is much better to have your children running outdoors, hanging from the trees, landscaping your yard beautifully, along with daddy, and building things, cooking, hiking, exploring, and inventing.

You *can* use just the computer *keyboard*, alone, for acquiring touch-typing skills when children are still very young. Just keep the screen off while working this typing speed up to 60-90 words per minute. (See our website for information regarding Zoom-Type.) This skill will make them ready to zoom to the top of the job market when the time comes, to say nothing of helping them to write more effectively through their school years. Far too many little ones crawl onto the computer to dink around hunting and pecking with games, etc. This produces bad neuron-networking that just has to get re-programmed the right way later on—when they begin to seriously learn to touch-type. Your children can power up the computer *after* they are able to touch-type 90 wpm.

With all these well-aimed tools/triggers, academics can return to their true godly foundations: a chance to grow, to better serve our fellow man, and to worship.

Try **reviewing** all of these academic triggers. Can you describe how each one works? Being able to confidently use them will make your teaching job easier and your children's experience with academics happier.

Part 4:

Top-Notch Home Management Strategies

Home management objective #1:
Stay near your fuel

There is a story of an old English gardener who lived in a little cottage near the Thames. He loved and tended his garden faithfully. Unfortunately, in his garden he had one grape vine that simply would not produce. Year in and year out its leaves were withered and sickly looking. He seriously considered cutting it down. But the appearance of a shriveled grape or two always made him hesitate.

However, one year he glanced at the grape vine and, much to his astonishment, he noted that it was covered with dozens of rich, succulent grapes, and the leaves were fully green, wrapping themselves strongly about the fence. The old gardener fell to his knees and quickly pawed at the undergrowth until he found the roots. He traced the tap root this way and that until he found himself on the bank of the Thames River. The little grape vine had found its fuel by plunging into the opulent waters of that huge river, and oh, what a difference it made in the fruit it could bear.

Likewise, we too need to stay near our fuel supply. Our fuel is spiritual, and it comes from Christ. Our emotional gas tanks are so small that we frequently run out, sometimes even between sentences. In a family it is so easy to gravitate toward becoming snarly and cranky with one another, if we hear no voice but our own. But just one glimpse of Jesus, one snatch of Scripture, lifts our spirits, extinguishes our desire to sin, softens our voices, and fills our eyes with the love of Jesus. Simply by looking at and hearing the words of one so holy, we are immediately changed.

> "We are children of God, and what we WILL BE has not yet been made known. But we know that when He appears, we shall be like Him…. Everyone who has THIS HOPE IN HIM PURIFIES HIMSELF, just as He is pure" (1 John 3:2-3).

 Because a mother's life is so filled with distractions, sleeplessness, and endless chores (scores of them, like freshly spilled milk, not even on the to-do list) it's important to live off of verses, even if one can only read them on the run. Better one verse, than no verse. One mother has arranged open Bibles all over the house so that she can read the Scriptures when she sits to nurse, or stands to change diapers, etc. She stays near her fuel.

One of the enemy's favorite tactics is to tell you that if you can't do a godly discipline thoroughly, then don't do it at all. The opposite is true: if we'll pray about every anxiety as it happens, crying out to God for wisdom in this tangled mess of relating and in that unexpected turn of events, the habit of prayer will turn into the love of prayer and the larger discipline of praying for longer periods of time will grow out of this fertile soil naturally.

A part of our hearts remains stony if we don't read Scripture AND pray. Scripture illumines our prayer, and prayer gives feet to the Scripture. If we settle for one over the other for days at a time, there is still ground in the heart that the LORD does not yet possess, and we'll find ourselves living far too frequently by our own wits, exhausted.

It takes two chemicals to make water to satisfy our thirst. So, too, the soul's access to spiritual fuel has two runways. If we only pray and don't pore over the Scripture, we're really not interested in His view of things. Conversely, if we only read Scripture and do not pray, subliminally it can sometimes mean that we feel estranged from God in a number of subtle areas. Perhaps, we've convinced ourselves that we can't pray, or that it would take too much time to pray the way we should, or that we're unworthy because in the PAST we haven't prayed as we ought. We come under the defeating suggestion of the enemy that we'll never be any better, so "why bother to pray at all?"

We should pray in spite of all these feelings because prayer releases the feeling of the life of heaven to us, minute by minute. Out of 10 minutes, how much better to spend three minutes in holy living, than all 10 in miserable hopelessness.

Better to experience this three-minute trickle of grace, knowing that it eventually leads to the fountain, than to flounder around in the desert and wind, with no let-up, because we won't pray at all.

I knew an old woman who practiced these two spiritual disciplines so well that she exuded the life of God as she generously served her large extended family. They all loved her. This grandmother delighted in going from house to house to serve her grown children's families (she didn't stop with just the first generation). She would do laundry and sort drawers and bake pies and bread and leave them all neatly in a line on the counter when she left. She would mend everyone's socks, too.

This grandma had been a fine cellist, frequently traveling to New York for lessons. She gave it all up to come home and serve her grown children's families and be a listening ear. She served so heartily that often she tumbled into bed late at night. One day after she had run children to their basketball practices, they even found her asleep at the steering wheel of the car, parked in her driveway. But amidst the sweeping and the making of quiche pies she sought nourishment at the feet of Jesus. She snatched a Scripture or a prayer frequently throughout the day. Every time I saw her read her Bible, it seemed like she was reading it as if this would be her last opportunity. She clung to every word, knowing that she had to make the brief moments count to the fullest—so that she could emerge from the reading and praying to live and give to the fullest.

When this grandma reached 90 she was nearly blind, but her spirit was still so beautiful, the grandchildren and great-grandchildren all wanted her around. They even continued to take her to basketball games. When she heard an uproar, she would lean over to a granddaughter and ask, "What just happened, honey?!" She was in the game of life to the end. She even lifted small one pound weights in the morning to keep herself fit until the LORD called her home. When that time came, she didn't change *OCCUPATIONS*—that of loving God and feeding off from Him—only *LOCATIONS*.

Stay near your fuel; life is impossible without it.

Home management objective #2:
Sharpen your focus

For a mother, time comes in two packages. The first is **reactionary time** (the second is discretionary time). In the early years, almost all of her time is taken up with responsiveness, reacting to the unpredictable. Even with nothing on her to-do list, her day is full of the sheer duty of maintenance (fixing the next meal, changing the diaper) or responding to unforeseen developments in the day as they transpire (cleaning up the spilled milk, comforting the child with the bee sting, patching up the conflict between siblings, mending the torn pants). In the later years, time gets eaten up with hours of unanticipated tactful psychological warfare with adolescents.

Since all of this time usage is unpredictable, the great challenge in managing this kind of time is not working harder at setting better goals, but rather working harder at *making time holy*: purposing to make lemonade out of lemons, learning how to better a situation by her composure, possessing a meek and quiet spirit, and influencing the atmosphere in positive directions as it passes. Your goal is to become a master at making time uplifting for the entire family. It's a tall order. Stampede the negative with the positive. Continually surround your family with an uplifting semantic atmosphere.

Each evening, evaluate how you're doing. Could your voice soften? Could you smile more? Are you able to turn around the entire volatile charged atmosphere by your own cheerfulness?

The second package that time comes in is **discretionary time**: bits of time early in the morning, or late at night or during nap time, whenever spare minutes present themselves. It is for these minutes that we need written goals. Just where are you headed? Where do you want to hurl your vigor, during the expanse of a lifetime? Distractions to that overarching goal are lethal. Most often, for each of us, the good becomes the enemy of the best. Probably the most promising aspect of goal setting is that it helps you to say a confident "No" to everything else. It might be nice to quilt, sort pictures, do crafts, and window-shop, but where does it get you, long-range, if you do? Staying in the pilot's seat requires having a cockpit of written goals from which to function.

Spend your discretionary time as if it were gold. Spend it with wisdom. Spend it in light of your tombstone—what do you want written on it? Most American women spend over 150 hours a year shopping for clothes but only one hour per year planning their life focus. Set some goals. (Set some goals for each child, too. What would you like to see them excel in this week?) Then, to further focus, take your own mile-long list of things you want to accomplish and prioritize that list. After you have completed this, then focus exclusively on your top goal each day. You may only stagger a little ways toward achieving your top goal in any given day, but steady application will finally get you there. When you start prizing your free minutes, you may find that some days will have several extra hours hidden in them.

One of the best ways for you to focus is to figure out what you are really good at and enjoy doing, and then improve it, tweak it, and plus it. Get better at refining it. Do it with jaw-dropping excellence. You'll be very fulfilled if you'll cooperate with your God-given wiring and appetites, and others will be blessed beyond your imagining. Most of us go through life suppressing all our God-given desire and drive, thinking everyone else is good at the same things. They're not. What rings YOUR bells may not even be on the map for the next person.

Here's a little illustration. A godly woman who lives in the countryside, not far from us, loves horses. She also uses her horses to bless others. She and her husband have adopted five children who all now ride. And she gives horseback riding lessons to scores of troubled children from the city.

She asked me one day, very excitedly, "Tell me the truth: does your head not turn at every horse you see as you drive through the country to my house?" I answered plainly

"Frankly, I don't even notice them." Hearing that, she grew a wee bit sad.

However, I answered her further and said, "Now you tell ME the truth. As you drive, does your head not turn at every front porch you see, perhaps imagining it repainted a more cheerful color and the furniture arranged more artfully with a teapot in the midst for more uplifting hospitality?" A bit downcast, she replied, "No, I never notice people's front porches." And then a look of understanding came to her eyes.

> You see, the thing *your* mind runs to may be a divine gift! It is important to identify that gift and find some way to serve with it.

One can observe that if there is a traffic accident, five people may arrive each with a different priority, concern or contribution. One may offer a blanket and hold the wounded head in her lap comforting the victim during shock; another may ask if she can call the insurance company; another may offer water; another will check out the car damage and offer their mechanical help or offer spare parts; and yet another will start controlling traffic around the scene of the accident.

You see, we are all motivated by different passions, and your particular "craziness" is unlike anyone else's, so sit up and take notice of what you're called to for the benefit of your family, your neighborhood, and the whole body of Christ.

Make sure that what you're drawn to is something that will benefit others. Self-absorption is never condoned in Scripture. If your first passion is stamp-collecting, maybe you'd better look further down in your soul for a second passion that will serve mankind and open a door for the gospel. You'll soon be at the great bar of the Judge of all the earth, giving an account of your time.

If your passion is making bread, get a more efficient apron and a more colorful basket. Your cheerful basket may be used to carry the bread to a sick person. Learn how to make three different kinds. Make them over and over until you're an expert. Get the proper cooking tools. Enclose a tract. Freeze some ahead so that the next time there's a mama sick in someone's home, you can arrive on the scene with a loaf ready-made.

If your skill is teaching children to read (and your own children are all older and can help you), get an old bus and travel to a poor section of the city, or areas where migrant workers congregate, and offer reading classes ON your bus. Remove the seats and add a colorful, comfortable carpet for the young learners to sit on, and bring phonics supplies. Advertise on the side of the bus that you offer free reading classes. As you grow to love the people, offer the LORD's salvation freely, too.

Working on needlepoint for your own chair doesn't cut it, unless you're doing it while you're doing something like waiting in the lobby for an elderly person you're transporting.

Avoid traps of business ventures, work situations, volunteer opportunities, church projects and family projects where you won't like the actual hour-by-hour things you'll be doing. Make sure that the end results you desire won't mean daily slavery in an area you dislike immensely. Cut your list of things you want to buy in half if acquiring more things submits you to types of work you loathe for protracted days, months, or years on end. It is important to live, to really thrive emotionally now, in fulfilling work. Therefore, spend some thought figuring out what that is, for you.

> "Each one should use *whatever gift he has received* to serve others, faithfully and administering God's grace in its various forms" (1 Peter 4:10).

Just a note here. For financial reasons and during some seasons of life it may not be possible to pursue what really rings your bells, but you can determine to use every spare moment to veer in that direction every time there *is* an opportunity until you eventually have more time. Well-set goals will deliver you from hours of trivial pursuits.

Goal setting that is done only in January and forgotten in February won't get you anywhere. Daily examination and rewriting, evaluation and course correction of your goals will put you into hyper drive. Knocking off that top priority written out every morning will yield amazing results. Know where you're going, buttress your resolve by staring at your words frequently, and get serious about focused use of all your discretionary time. Grab the moments when the house is quiet to work on your mental plans, saving your maintenance chores for when there is noise and a crowd around.

The chief end of man is to glorify God and to enjoy Him forever. Target your life for financial solvency and evangelism (beginning with the discipleship of your own children) within that larger goal. Keeping this view consistently in mind produces good mental health.

When you struggle inwardly at times comparing yourself with others with futile thoughts like: "Why do they have all the children? "Why does he or she get all the attention?" or "Why do they get all the financial breaks?" just readjust your view of the contest of life. All envy and jealousy will disappear from your mind if you'll focus on your own job of prevailing prayer and drawing souls closer to their Maker. Improve the way that you can serve others with excellence for your Master's sake. Make these things the slow, quiet occupation of your inner man, and you won't have time or energy to compare yourself with anyone.

Home management objective #3:
Strive for a simplified life

Ask of every purchase and every activity: "What does this commit me to in the future? Does it center our life as a family or will it splinter it?"

The single most important thing you can do to simplify your life is to **stop shopping as a pastime**. Our culture is out of control in this area. Materialism keeps you going after trappings rather than essences—having to have more and more sets of dishes rather than serving a better and better meal, even if it is in plastic dishes. We are the largest consumers in the world, and we still want more. Shopping is enervating and is counterproductive to every goal you've written down. The sheer detailed decision-making it requires is tiring; the discontent it breeds is subconsciously emotionally taxing; the internal conflict over the unplanned money it will require is stressful; and the wasted time produces regret. When you return home, you realize that some needful chore was left undone and no dent was made in your big picture of accomplishing your goals. If you can view shopping as an enemy to your own advancement and a robber of your own vital energy and time for someone *else's* pocketbook, you gain the muscle needed to break a defeating habit.

Try running errands only once a week for groceries and bare necessities, or get in the habit of waiting to grab needful items only if you have to go to town for an appointment anyway. See how swiftly you can descend upon a store to get only the genuinely needed items on your list and get back out again, without a single extra item. Focus on becoming a producer rather than a consumer. Think of the focused prolific lifetime production of Bach and Rembrandt. Be aware of which dog you're feeding in your insides. Contentment means rest for your nervous system. Do not darken the door of stores unnecessarily and you'll starve the dog of discontent.

One great saint said on his deathbed that the acquisition of more and more things was like so much "licking the earth." The real truth about acquiring things is that it will take energy to go buy the thing, energy to use the thing, energy to store, dust and clean the thing, and energy to eventually figure out how to get rid of the thing.

A second way to simplify your life is to **avoid external taskmasters you don't need**. You are your own best taskmaster. You know what to do with your life, based on your written goals. It's going to take  focused energy to get you there. Stay disentangled from others' expectations of you. Ask of new activities, how many extra rehearsals does this commit our family to? How many practices? How long will we chase this ball? Or ride this horse? Dance this jig? To what end? Divert your children's attention to suffering, unevangelized humanity, rather than preoccupation with gerbils, cats and dogs. Help them prefer to use their time to be rich in good deeds to *people*. Work together on projects that will bless and evangelize the needy. Keep focused on the big picture. Earthly diversions are many, strong, and tantalizing. To keep yourself focused on eternity, you'll need more than a moderate resolve.

So, become an expert at seeing external unexpected taskmasters a mile off and avoid getting hooked. Watch out for taskmasters that will extract a pound of your flesh and give very little in return. And avoid taskmasters that seem important now but may contribute very little to your overall later life.

For example, beware of a fund-raising drive for a not-so-worthy cause, extra 4-H projects that swallow up too much time, too many long phone calls that someone else initiates. Here's one for you: a youth group director gave each child a guppy floating in a little cardboard box as a gift on their way out the door. That gift cost the mothers no end of time and money buying all of the essentials needed to take care of this wee little gift, glass bowls, food, daily assignment of feeding chores, breaking up possessive quarrels over the one fish by six siblings, etc. Say "Thanks, but no thanks." Gifts that you have to return for a different size or color may eat up hours phoning, repackaging for shipping or driving—all over an object that you were living just fine without the day before. Could you use those hours for something nobler? Perhaps giving it away is a better use of time than making it perfect for you. Ask yourself repeatedly, "Is this where I really want to spend my time, or am I responding to someone else's agenda for me?"

Beware of impulsive distractions coming from your own head, too. Flower gardens that commit you to hours and hours of weeding you hadn't expected. Fabric on sale that commits you to sewing it up. You may want to turn away from a sale on mangoes that commits you to hours of canning you hadn't planned on. Or money-makers that involve too much sweat equity for too small of an outcome, too many lessons, craft projects that could easily and cheaply be bought instead of made. A boat that commits you to water several states away. Each of these may be well and good in their season and time, but just be sure you are deliberately deciding to do them. Would you choose these activities right now, over *all* the options available to you as a Christian, if you took the time to compare them to your long-range goals? "Why do that which someone else can or will do when there is so much to be done that someone else cannot or will not do" (said by Dawson Trotman, first president of The Navigators).

A third way to simplify your life is to **minimize enervating media input**, whether it's the evening news, sports events, or even wholesome movies. Three hours may be whisked away unnoticed, over and over. You'll never see those hours again, and the sheer bulk of your influence in the world will be diminished bit by bit by this apparently good but quietly consistent robber. You'll find your emotions fruitlessly exercised over issues or dilemmas you can do nothing about. Media input can leave you tired, not invigorated. When the media successfully captivates your attention, it means someone somewhere was denied your attention. The illusion is that you've done something when in actuality you've made no difference in the world.

By the way, never allow computers, video games and television in your children's bedrooms or you'll live to regret the day. All your careful good input will be supplanted via the more powerful evil media input. In addition, media truncates the  thought life because it presents information in frantic flashes. Contextual, mature thinking becomes less and less possible.

Use your spare time to illumine your mind with top quality reading material. Read the Bible, biography, history, science, and how-to books. Keep in mind that most fiction will not increase your skills or your service to mankind. As already mentioned, sometimes fiction (in whatever form) can take your emotions down a futile path. By the way, you may have to select your books conscientiously from trustworthy sources, as most modern public libraries progressively sell off the older books that promoted conservative values. The children's section of a library can be a dangerous place. Some of the new children's books are filled with scenarios involving the occult, serial marriages, immorality, and abandoned and abused children. (See our website to download Melanie's suggestions of excellent books.)

Learn to recognize that over-commitment, over-extension, protracted frenetic activity, endless media noise and talk shows can be the number one enemy of your soul. The soul finds its absolute best repose and renewing nourishment in prayer. Now think how little we pray. Our souls are more crinkled up than corn flakes. Being needlessly over-busy is the surest path to going berserk. The life of our soul degenerates if we don't avail ourselves of the spiritual discipline and forced piety of a complete Sabbath rest (one day in seven) and daily prayer and Bible reading.

And finally, stay home as much as possible. Build memories in your own house and in your own backyard. Establish open-ended home activities with which the family can become more and more proficient. Practicing musical instruments, improving hospitality (it says of Job in the Bible that there was no one in the entire countryside who hadn't had meals in his home), ever-improving athletic ability: longer and more vigorous walks, more demanding rebounding, stretching, weight lifting (all at home). As a family you could grow organic produce and build more and more beautiful landscaping outside the home—more pathways, waterfalls—until you have your own little Garden of Eden and baby trees are planted and named after your own babies, to grow along with them.

By the way, did I mention stay home yet? Strive not to raise your children in your car, trapped under a seat belt. "The wise woman is to be busy *at home*" (Titus 2:5). Intimate exchanges most often happen in the context of the luxury of lots of relational time. The non-believer lives from event to event (frenetic activity). The believer lives in the bosom of a relationship. "In Him we live and move and have our being" (Acts 17:28). Our homes foster this better than our malls.

Home management objective #4:
Get financially solvent *today*.
Don't wait 'til tomorrow!

Debt produces stress. The bigger the debt, the more stress. Like a bloodhound on a trail, work intensely to eliminate your debt. Long-range "tomorrow" solutions will keep you in bondage, so figure out how you can rearrange your life today to eliminate it all (including your house mortgage). No amount of scrimping and saving will do for you what significantly living under your means will do. Therefore, begin by lowering your standard of living. Think "downward mobility" for upward ease of spirit. Avoid financial leaks by limiting being in and around stores. Teach your children that they don't get the whole dollar, when they earn one. Get them in the habit of removing tithe and tax money from their earnings, and then saving the bulk of it for their own debt-free car and home someday.

Once you've lowered the costs of your housing situation as far as possible, go after the rest of your debt load by

(1) selling off excess, (2) buying nothing but bare necessities (stop buying), (3) saving, and (4) earning more around the edges, perhaps by picking up extra work or developing entrepreneurial sources of income. Make sure that your entrepreneurial ventures, however, are cash producers from day one, not cash eaters. Otherwise, abandon them. (5) Tithe faithfully. You desperately need God's help, and this is the avenue by which He'll release circumstantial favor to you. Also: before you go shopping, get caught up on your bookkeeping and recheck your budget—you'll spend less when you do go.

So, your two primary financial goals are 1) to get mortgage-free at your earliest possible hour and then 2) to move on to finding some source of additional steady monthly *extra* in-come, that *you* control, not your boss/job. You want to focus on setting this up so that you won't have to work for someone else anymore when you are older. If you accrue savings, think about investing in your own extra business, not the volatile stock market. Invest the extra instead of spending extra. "Plant your corn; don't eat your corn!" Invest in your own, on the side, business to get it to the place where someone else can run it for you and/or you can duplicate it somewhere else.

If you opt to build your own business, don't overextend yourself. Pay as you go; delay hiring help (except for your own children) for as long as you can. After protecting your business idea legally, test the market, try it out in a few close neighborhoods, or try selling a few prototypes first before you invest substantial money in developing scores of them. Keep a tight grip on your expenses. Grow slowly, from strength to strength. Work out the kinks in a small set-ting/on a small scale first.

If you invest in real estate (using cash only), your own home included, try to keep up any and all of your real estate property and grounds well. It protects the largest invest-ment you probably have, by increasing its resale value. Curb appeal can land you a sale. By the way, when improving the aesthetics of any property, try to use free things: save your money for functional things.

Beware of wanting to become richer and richer. "Does it make you a king to have more and more cedar?" (Jeremiah 22:15). What is the end result that you are after? Is it to be able to put your feet up while sitting by a river? Just go do that now! "If I were only rich" can have a price tag of wearying responsibility.

Debt-filled financial stress will keep you hung up and strung up. It will keep you from really experiencing life as God meant for you to live it. It will hammer and tong you all the way into depression. Jettison it as rapidly as you can figure out how to. Don't leave any stone unturned.

Home management objective #5:
Build your body for the long haul

Imagine you're age 16 and you've been given a car—only one—to last your entire lifetime. You will never have another. How would you treat that car? You probably wouldn't run right out and fill the gas tank with ice cream! Over time the upholstery might tear and the paint may chip, but keeping the car functioning optimally is your chief concern. As you know, the thing that affects that function the most is the type of fuel you choose each and every time you fill it. Also, you know that longer weekly drives in the country will clean out the carburetor and serve a car better than endless stop-and-go city driving.

If we would do all this for our car, then why don't we eat properly and exercise to keep our bodies fit for the long haul? Perhaps it is because when we're young, we really don't believe we'll ever lose our health. We should make it a habit to look at the elderly, to really look hard, and ask, "Do I want to end up like that?" We all grow old, but today, 99% develop needless chronic degenerative diseases WHILE they age, simply because of what they've placed on the ends of their forks.

Research has shown beyond a shadow of a doubt that the premium food needed for optimal nutrition is raw (enzyme-rich) fruits and vegetables, nuts and seeds. The Surgeon General says it, the scientific reviews say it, the  *Journal of the American Medical Association* says it, the FDA says it, copious health books say it, and history says it. Cured cancer patients say it.

With every fork-full, ask yourself: "Is this raw? Is this a fruit? Is this a vegetable? Is this a nut? Is this a seed?" If it isn't both raw and one of those four choices, it is a small vote lost for having the ultimate health possible while you're still a mortal! If every morsel passes these questions, history has shown in case after case that the individuals who are eating like that are living to be 110, 115, 117, while retaining their vigor! The amount of research is staggering now that it is primarily diet that affects your disease-rate, not unavoidable germs, as was thought before. If your diet is top-notch, so will be your immune system. Clogging arteriosclerotic materials simply cannot be manufactured out of this fuel. Your risk for a heart attack while eating this way is nil. Dazzling synthetics and lifeless dead cooked food don't deliver any nutrition. They are a waste of digestive energy. Just add more raw today. Every time you snack, make it raw.

Health is a four-legged chair upon which you may sit with confidence. If any leg is broken, all bets are off. The legs are raw enzyme-rich food, spiritual life (John 3:16), adequate water, and exercise. A daily three-mile brisk walk, drinking half your weight in ounces of water each day, rebounding with weights, and stretching will deliver the sunshine and oxygen-load needed to sustain lifetime health. Cancer cells cannot live in oxygen. Toxicity only feeds on dead materials. Your daily strategy is to starve off (with only live foods) and kill off (with a mother lode of oxygen) any mincing toxic invasion. You can't afford *not* to spend time exercising.

You simply must find a way to build the mental heat up high enough to make these daily choices, one day at a time. You're no good to anyone if you're listless and enervated for the last 40 or so years of your life. If need be, earn less money, do fewer activities, make fewer commitments, volunteer less, and go fewer places. Gird yourself to take the time to invest in your 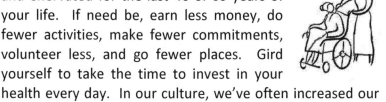 health every day. In our culture, we've often increased our speed to cover for the fact that we've lost our way.

Rearrange your priorities to invest in a healthy physical body for the long haul. It took some of us 30 years to get these priorities right.

Financial wisdom is gained either by taking someone else's wise words for how it is achieved or viscerally by feeling your cheek against the pavement the first night you are homeless. It is the same with health. You can either believe the voluminous research and act upon it today, or wait until you feel the first breakdown of some spot in your body you didn't even know you had, and then scramble like mad, hoping against hope that it's not runaway. Daily prevention is far less painful. Self-indulgence has its price tag.

Home management objective #6:
Prize your primary duty

Family meals

Whether you're naturally the domestic type or not, you must become domestic when you're the mother of a family. Run toward the tasks that you dislike instead of shirking them and you'll find a strange new spiritual vigor grow up inside of you. Conforming to any Biblical mandate has a silver lining you can't see when you are just beginning.

The primary way motherhood is demonstrated (expressed) and received (understood) is through the feeding of your family. A family is fed in two ways: (1) with nurturing *words* and (2) with nurturing *food*. The mother feeds her family all

day long with uplifting, encouraging, loving words. She provides a semantic atmosphere that actually sustains the emotional life of the whole home. Her words are a safe haven, a
sheltered beach, a refurbishing point, a continual domestic
fountain of inspiration and enabling.

Equally important is the delivery of wholesome nutritious food
for the stomach. As a mother you're engaged in providing
food for others from the womb to the tomb. You might as
well saddle in and not only get used to it, but work at improving your delivery. Since it must be done, the only way to enjoy
it is to improve the way you do it. Running out to meet your
meal preparations ahead of time removes the fear and dread
of having to do it at all. Far too many modern mothers are
surprised by the arrival of dinnertime.

If meal preparation does not stay your highest priority
through the years of raising a family, your household will
suffer by little degrees and by big. Many women trade meal
preparation hours for decorating, phone calls, crafts, picture
sorting, continuing education classes, etc., while their families
face dashed expectations, meal after meal. The family eventually silently gives up hoping, and a vital part of family life
dies. Health degenerates, too, as the family is reduced to less
than optimum choices and hunger drives them to downright
addictive choices.

So, see to it that before proceeding on any personal project,
sewing, reading, friendly phone calls, writing, music, sports,
etc., you've made sure your family's food is all prepared for
the entire day, the grocery shopping is done for the morrow,
the house is fully cleaned and picked up, and that you are up
to date with all your financial accounting (all bills paid, all

receipts for expenses recorded). Then and only then can you be at leisure to pursue personal projects without adding additional stress to both yourself and your family. Strangely, one of the biggest stress reducers for *you* is to meet your family's needs first. No one can live with such efficiency all the time because of unforeseen interruptions, but returning to these priorities as quickly as possible, after the interruption, will reduce your stress load dramatically.

If you don't believe how important this is, observe the smiles and lit up eyes every time you do set a good meal before your family. It is a family's birthright to expect to be fed. (They *can* help, once they see that you are in command of the big picture.) You nurtured your children in the womb and at the breast; your anatomy is strong evidence that you were created to carry on with the task. In turn, your family's grateful expressions and glad faces will feed you back.

If you don't make meal preparation the most important work of the day and only when it is finished turn to other tasks, it will come down upon you like a house of cards, mealtime after mealtime. The stress-free avenue is advanced preparation. "A good cook always has one foot in the next meal." Realize that meal preparation takes time. Protect that time. Give your best energy to it, not your worst. Pray for it to become important to you. Pray to "view your kitchen sink as an altar rather than an obstacle" (words of Elisabeth Elliot). Pray for God to help you with ideas when you feel bankrupt and out of steam. Begin to do it with excellence. Finesse both your cooking preparation skill and your delivery.

An optimal strategy is to do all your food preps first thing in the morning. If your family is older and doesn't need you every minute, you can listen to inspiring tapes while working. This can help you actually look forward to your preparations. You'll want to prepare healthy snacks and bottle purified water for your family to consume in the car while running errands or while they work at their jobs. If your family is largely committed to eating fresh and raw, that means working a day ahead of when the food will be eaten. At night you'll start soaking all the next day's nuts, seeds, grains. This begins the digestive process in the food itself and makes them far easier to digest in the stomach. Set out any frozen foods needed for the next day. They will thaw out, making them easy to grind with spices and hot water for a delicious nearly raw enzyme rich soup for lunch. Cut and slice fruits and veggies for the day in the morning. As you grow in these skills it will take less and less mental energy in the future.

As long as we're on earth this is necessary work, vital work, rewarding work. See to it that you consistently give it your best time and your best energies. It doesn't take a *long* time each day, but it does take *some* time, so adjust your woman-hood around it. If you do, your family will rise up and call you blessed.

Develop the skill of sewing

Every home needs a seamstress. If you want your family to LOOK orderly, neat, well-groomed and modest for the glory of God, you'll find that necessary alterations are needed for everyone's clothes all through the years. Either you or your older daughters need to incrementally become progressively proficient as a seamstress. This is a skill that you can easily acquire by using small moments wisely.

Every woman who can *both* cook and sew brings added blessing to any home, just like a man does who can do small maintenance jobs around the home, over a man who only plays video games. There is no glory in *not* being able to do domestic skills. There is no downside to increasing our capabilities for serving others all the way into old age, either. Determine to become skilled in as many ways as possible.

You can train yourself in 10-minute sessions via sewing books as well as actually *doing* your sewing/alteration sessions in 10-minute intervals. Having a small sewing area permanently and efficiently set up will allow you to quickly fix/mend/alter things in and around other necessary domestic tasks. If this is a new skill for you, we offer a DVD of simple easy alterations to get you going, as well as a beginner's sewing booklet that can be ordered at our website.

For all alterations, Mary Roehr's *Altering Woman's Ready to Wear* and *Altering Men's Ready to Wear* are excellent reference books with clear simple pictures and easy to read text. If you want private tutoring in sewing, contact us.

Prepare your own alternative natural pharmacy

As the woman of your home, you are most often your family's nurse, too. In that role, are you becoming sick and tired of making too many trips to the doctor's office? Discouraged with the side effects of drugs? Want a way out? There is a way out of much of that, by using essential oils.

You can "nurse" *capably* with oils. Oils get results. They have pulled my own family out of no end of health challenges, and today we simply would not be without them. There isn't a day that goes by that we don't use them for something or other.

God put healing oils in plants that mankind might draw them out and use them. Trees have been given for the healing of the nations (Revelation 22:2). Essential oils are loaded with healing energy, rare and numerous chemical compounds that often function better than antibiotics, and mother-loads of oxygen. There was a reason why frankincense and myrrh were brought to the Christ-child as some of the earth's highest treasures 2,000 years ago.

We have been using oils for over 15 years and have—in our first years—wasted years and money on inferior oils sold in health food stores. Many of those oils were jerked out of plants using solvents (substances that are foreign to our bodies). And many of these oils have *not* been extracted at the optimal hours for the oil's particular and specific max-imal therapeutic molecular activity, either. Not all oils are equal.

You can become an expert in the use of oils overnight by using an *Essential Oils Desk Reference*. Growing a strong knowledge of essential oils will make you the agency of re-lieving suffering in the lives of many people, not the least of which is your own family.

Acquiring oils is some of the best health insurance you could have, too. It is good to have them as a pharmacy of your own—not only for everyday, but for emergency preparation, as well. When and if the power goes out, or gasoline runs out, what you have in your own home will be all that is available. If you are interested, contact us and we can tell you more "ins and outs" of using essential oils.

Home management objective #7:
Handle your house well

> **The sure road to relief: improve the way you do it all!**

Since maintenance of a home in all its details won't go away—*somebody* has to do it (your children will help, of course, but the buck stops with you)—the only relief you'll get is if you seek to *improve* **the way you do it all**! Make it a private game with yourself and the tyranny of it will go away. Instead of running from it, tackle it. Engage yourself in a mind-game of an "improve-a-thon" and you'll grow incredibly polished and capable in domestic skill. Work at little ways to shave your minutes in all your domestic pursuits with jobs that you do over and over. Look for ways to conquer reoccurring domestic problems and functions. And relentlessly look, like Sherlock Holmes, for ways to do it easier.

Become a queen of your total domain. Enjoy your kingdom. Enjoy managing it, much like the president of a large corporation, making it exactly as you want it, lovingly stewarding it under God to the best of your ability. It has been said that: "*an institution is really the lengthened shadow of the man at the top.*" So, too, is a home. The woman establishes the climate in incalculable ways.

If you really get into it, you'll join the ranks of keepers at home who realize that they have one of the loveliest, most varied and interesting jobs on the planet. Think of the countless women in China who work in a warehouse attaching the same widget hour after hour every day for years on end. Come to see homemaking as the blessing God intended, and count yourself fortunate.

Brave bold bulldozing

> *Principle:* **Spend a lot of time now conquering each and every department of your home so that you can spend less time later.**

Take dominion and refine each area. Act like you are in college and the task of conquering your home is your final semester's project that will determine your course grade. Approach your home like a Ph.D. candidate. Become a Pretty-Hefty-Duty mom who tells those slippery domains to conform or else!

Here are some of a home's departments to *rein in* and *reign over*:

- Deep cleaning schedule setup that includes refrigerator, stove, pantry, etc., as well as beginning a companion habit of working on one of those larger chores a day.

- Main living areas: visually appealing and homey; enough comfortable chairs for guests; pleasant pictures on the walls; and an inviting front door (order our *Home Staging Tips* e-book/Kindle book #108 for much more on this topic).
- Kitchen cupboards and counters arranged, sorted to maximize efficiency.
- Backup supplies of food and paper products.
- Hospitality preparations well thought-out ahead of time and easily accessible, ready to implement at a moment's notice.
- Linens: sorted and neatly folded, with adequate supplies.
- Everyone's closets, conquered.
- Homeschooling materials shelved and labeled for each child; non-current materials in labeled boxes.
- Cars: clean and well maintained, including a car maintenance record for each vehicle and a tickler system for oil changes, etc.
- Accounting receipts etc., organized in file folders—a place for everything and everything in its place; up-to-date logbook of monthly finances. (For more, see our booklet #s 63 and 5, respectively, on managing your family papers and finances.)

Bottom line: get organized. You simply don't have time to go on being unorganized. Being organized *saves* you time. You can grab things quicker and reduce dislocation stress as everyone yells at each other, trying to find even the most basic of things (pencil, papers, shoes, scarves, mittens, keys).

Fix up, finalize, and publicize the correct place for everything. Begin with labeled cardboard records storage boxes, if you need to; they're far cheaper than buying furniture. The ones with removable lids are a dream to handle.

Use meal times as a short leash. Right before everyone sits at the table, you can say, "Let's look around the room: is everything back in its place?" For everyone's sake, train each child to put away each thing he finishes before he is allowed to pull out the next thing.

The organization of your home won't be conquered in a day. But we can hope it **will be so** after six months of steady focus. Year after year of chaos begins to define a childhood. Give your child the habit of order for his own future life, by the pleasant memory of it in his childhood home.

Linen enhancement

We met a woman who told us her career was working in Linen Enhancement. Having never heard of such a career, we probed further. She laughed and said that she did laundry for a hotel.

So, how can we enhance those linens—how can we manage that department better?

Regarding bedding: work toward having two sets of sheets for each bed, even if you have to start with thrift store ones. Since your children sleep in pajamas, you usually only need to change their sheets every other week, but change the pillowcases weekly.

When you *do* change sheets, try to make it a habit to remake the beds with the clean set right away, when your energy levels are highest. If you delay to put the clean set on, often it gets put off 'til bedtime when everyone is far crankier and has way less energy to face it. Later in the day, after you've finished the laundry, put your freshly laundered set of sheets back into the linen closet. This ensures that you are always rotating your sheets, not wearing out one set more than another.

When thinking about your sheet purchases, try to color coordinate the sheets with the mattress size. Also, designate different shelves in your linen closet, marked for each size bed. Sheets that have some blue in them might be for the single beds, the cream colored ones for the double beds, etc.; that way you don't have to unfold every sheet to figure out which bed it is for.

Airing out beds every morning is a good idea. Toxins are eliminated every night through respiration as we sleep, so in the morning throw back the covers clear to the bottom of the bed, air the room out with fresh air, and make the beds up after breakfast. Have your children learn to air out their jammies, too, before stuffing them back in a drawer all wadded up. They can be taught to lay them over a chair or the bed near the window, neatly, 'til after breakfast.

Corral your domestic spaces

Some of you are raising large families in very cramped quarters. Others of you are living in huge areas, veritable barns, but they seem cold and uninviting. Let's talk about conquering spaces—not outer space, but inner space—and creating homey spaces.

(1) If you have too little space: If you only have a dinky kitchen to work in, think of French chefs. They have historically worked in dinky spaces, too. Think of the wonderful cuisine they were able to produce in such tight places. That is where the idea of hanging all your kitchen equipment from the ceiling came from. The advantage of small kitchens is that you can grab everything by pivoting on one foot. Learn to be grateful for that! Attitude is everything.

In addition to that splendid idea of *hanging* pots and pans, if you occasionally need to achieve more **counter** space, grab pre-cut boards and place them on open kitchen drawers. Cut Plexiglas™ or 1/4 inch plywood into rectangles to lay on top of these drawers when needed and opened. Store these thin boards standing up in the crack between your fridge and cupboard, to have them close by and ready to retrieve at a moment's notice to give you more production space. Cut the wood or Plexiglas™ exactly the size to fit the top of each drawer that you want to double use in this manner. To get the size exactly right, try cutting each one out of cardboard first, so that each final board sits on top and doesn't fall down into its drawer.

If your kitchen's *eating* area is too small, turn your kitchen table into permanent additional *counter* space—creating a larger work area—and move your actual eating into the dining room or double-use your living room space for meals.

To achieve more space in the rest of your house, you have to think like an inch-engineer. Consider affixing tiny narrow shelves on the walls behind all of your doors. Raise all of your beds on plastic bed leg risers (available at many department stores), using the space underneath for boxes or plastic containers. Make all desks only 18 inches deep and use the wall in front of and above each desk for all the stuff that you normally stash on the back half of any desk. Go UP. If you think about it, people only actually work on the front half of their desks. If you have to go really far up to gain enough space, hang a lightweight folding two-step ladder close by.

(2) If you have too much space: Group your seating arrangements into cozy little areas around smaller area rugs. Have various areas designated for specific different activities, with large hallways or passageways in between, even going right through the center of a room. Cultivate closeness for your family. When arranging chairs, try out a real conversation. Does it feel close and stress free, or do you find yourselves yelling to communicate or stretching to share a book's pictures?

When you have lots of space, use all of it. Set up a homemade massage table, a ping-pong table, chess sets, an indoor bowling area with beach balls, an easel and painting center, exercise equipment, charts on the walls, world maps, white boards, etc.

In large spaces, liberally place end tables near all chairs and couches to set books and lamps upon. If money is tight you can toss a pretty piece of fabric over several stacked cardboard boxes to make end-tables at no expense. Remember, your home will be hallmarked with books, so provide plenty of bookcases. (Narrow bookcases can be placed down hallways or even behind doors.) Take a child who has read 500 profound books and stand him next to a child who has seen 500 trite movies and the difference between those two children is staggering—like two different creatures from two different planets.

Whether your living space is provokingly small or bizarrely large, as an innovative flexible mother you can say along with the Apostle Paul, "I've learned in whatsoever state I'm in, therewith to *make my family* content!" (paraphrased very loosely).

Upgrade later

Conquer your homes systems/functions at the lowest expedient levels first. Just concentrate on getting your entire household to function smoothly. Reward yourself with the thought that you can always upgrade later. If you don't have dressers, use cardboard boxes; if you don't have cardboard boxes, use sacks. If you don't have front and back door mats, use cardboard. If you don't have enough dish towels, tear up an old bath towel. If you don't have good books for your children and can't afford them, buy a used old encyclopedia set at the thrift store for $5 and have them read *that* for a while. If your young children don't have the right clothes for all occasions, take huge seams up the backs of older people's used clothes. If you don't have gorgeous art for your home, hang up beautiful towels or sheets. Get your home *feeling* like a home and *functioning* like a home on *some* level from the get-go. Even if you live in a van or a tent, *organize* it. Have hooks and hangers for everything; attach things underneath the van or tent, out the back of the van or tent, on the roof of the van or tent.

If you don't have a guest room, figure out some way to slide the foot of one bed under another bed, or put a bed up near the ceiling, if you have to. Put hooks on the wall behind every door, if the closets are too stuffed. Put L brackets on long boards to make shelves, high up, one foot from the ceiling down all your hallways, if you need to.

Anticipate every need, every event. What will you need to make it go smoothly? Use your free time to conquer your home at deeper and deeper levels and at more efficient levels before taking more strolls down the malls or making social phone calls.

Learn to love your home and being *at* home. Learn to prefer it. Learn to love to manage your home. Learn how much fun it is to make it just exactly right. Arrange it so that nothing could possibly happen in your home that would ever throw you for a loop, logistically. Pre-think everything. It is *your* home. Take hold of it. Remember the joyful slogan: "I can always upgrade later."

Diffuse the huge

Each of us has things in our lives that we wish we would make ourselves do and simply can't get the old body to cooperate with. We foot-drag terribly—sometimes worse than our children do. We know we need to exercise consistently or pray more or daily make a big huge salad to improve our heath, or tackle arranging those family pictures, or clean the closets. We make high resolves that never happen.

With any discipline or any overwhelming project that we know we SHOULD conquer, the pattern for most of us is to psyche ourselves to hit it hard. We succeed on the first day, but that is usually followed by a corresponding crash for the rest of the week or month or year!

How 'bout trying the opposite approach?! Why not try incremental conquerings? For example: exercise just five  minutes, but do it *all* this week. Or just do three push-ups while standing up, pushing off a wall—but do it every day, all this week. Mark it on the calendar. Reward yourself at the end of the sixth day with something you never get to do much of, like reading for 10 minutes, or hiding in a closet and completely finishing one thought of your own, or something phenomenal like that. Then next week up it to 10 minutes every day. Mark that on the calendar. Grow a discipline like the tortoise did, rather than opt for the crash and burn approach of the hare.

In putting yourself under new management to acquire this new habit, you have to engage in a kind of sequential suicide by dropping everything to just go do it. You can kind of even rev yourself up by doing war hoops like those bobsled teams do in the Olympics before they all jump into the narrow box to shoot down 50 stories in a minute. Try leading with your body, short-circuiting the slower rational planning section of your brain. Just plop your feet out of the front door to go for your walk once a day. Ask "why?" only when you are out on the road with a half a mile already behind ya'! Or reach out your hands to sort the closet and drag your brain and sluggish emotions along *after* your actions.

Just take one little menacing area, one little area of guilt, one "dive and cover" topic, and apply yourself to it for five minutes. Break through inertia with creeping baby steps. Coach yourself with a little activity in that direction, followed by a lot of lavish praise. "Way ta go! Did you see *that*?! I actually made a dent in the thing!!!!!!!!!"

By the way, here's a suggestion about family picture albums. Forget it. Just slide those mountains of pictures into album sleeves as soon as they are printed. Pencil in the dates on the back of the pictures before they go into the sleeves— and call it quits. I know moms who have shoeboxes full of pictures that never get sorted, because they are waiting to do the million dollar work-up of the best family album ever. Or, you could assign the job to your children and take what you get!

For some huge jobs, the best strategy is **just not to care**. Resist being the hare OR the tortoise; instead, go sit in your favorite chair and read to your child or enjoy a good book yourself. There is nothing in the Ten Commandments that says you *have* to do family albums, polish silverware, or train your children to speak Arabic! If God didn't require it, why should you?! Often we tie ourselves up like Lazaruses with our own expectations. Sometimes *we* make life far more difficult than it needs to be.

Sort and pitch

Get rid of all excess stuff. There are simply whole trash cans full of stuff that you don't need sitting around your house, basement and garage. All of this stuffed, wedged, stockpiled para- phernalia weighs you down subconsciously. Sorting down external material possessions stashed on shelves, in boxes, cupboards, drawers and filing  cabinets has a profound impact on your psyche. When you get control of it, it serves to narrow down and define where you are actually going in life. It is a physical way to get you focused emotionally on what's important in your life. For maximum, immediate freedom, commit to doing it for 15 minutes each day as your highest priority (after preparing your day's meals) and stick with it 'til it's completed, even if it takes months. Eliminate and concentrate. De-junk and de-clutter.

Keep this de-junking principle in mind if you are considering any further decorating of your home. Consider only buying pictures that you hang on the wall, instead of three-dimen- sional objects. Pictures are flat. Translation? No dusting! 3D objects like statues, dried flowers, puffed pillows, etc.—each has to be dusted. Well-chosen large wall pictures powerfully set a mood for each room. They simply give the best bang for your buck. Avoid the 3D "cutsies" if you want to save yourself needless ongoing work.

Get a grip on your closet

Wear all of your clothes and all of your shoes, in order, each day, proceeding from one end of the closet to the other. Put something on tomorrow and each day after that you haven't worn for years. You'll know immediately what to do with it. If it needs mending, taking up, or letting out, do that now. Make the dress wearable today or get rid of it. You'll reduce your nine-foot rack of clothes down to two feet and you'll end up with more actually wearable clothes than you have ever owned. Surprisingly, your single most important criterion for clothing is what color it is. That is what your family sees constantly. You can look dynamite in second-hand clothes if the color makes you seem to have more energy. You don't see yourself as your family does. Forget about wearing white skirts or dresses or uncomfortable clothes, you can't work and serve in them. Think modesty too. Look in the mirror after dressing and bend different directions to see what shows.

Wear all your shoes, too. Put on a pair you haven't worn in a while (there's a reason why you haven't worn them—maybe you just haven't admitted it to yourself yet) and if you find you are taking them off in an hour, give them away. Proceed to the next pair until you find them too uncomfortable, and do like-wise. To quote a Scottish lady, the two or three pair you have left remaining are your dependable "substantial under-pinnings"! The others just took up space.

In planning your wardrobe, the easiest strategy is to have eight different outfits that each say something totally different, and then rotate wearing them. This cycle enables you never to wear the same thing on the same day of the week, in case you have repeating meetings always on Monday. Hang each outfit with all its parts together. Less is more. Simpler is better. Fewer clothes—less overall hassle.

Become a systems scrutinizer

"The wise woman looks *well* to the ways of her household" (Proverbs 31:27). This is not a casual endeavor. Apply yourself to it. Think through the details of all the systems in your home. Is this the best place to put this? Is this the best thing to use? Start looking objectively at what actually happens physically throughout the day in your home. What are the traffic patterns? Where do people toss their coats and shoes when they're passing through the front and back doors? Where do people put books and magazines when they're sitting and reading? Where do they stash their paperwork? Then build shelves, arrange little tables, and position wastebaskets and lamps around the places where the household living actually happens. Is there a more optimal way to park the car for bringing in groceries? By altering an outdoor path or driveway or removing an indoor wall or a cupboard that blocks a view, you can refresh and optimize all of your living conditions. Is a drawer or cupboard better used for these items than those currently occupying that space? Is this the most efficient use of all space and objects in your home? For anything that happens *repeatedly* in your home, have it happen *optimally*.

Mayors of cities

If you view your home just as a place to crash, you'll move from chaos to chaos, as the years pass and the number of children you birth increases. But if you'll view your home as a very important place, a veritable city over which you are the mayor, you'll move from order to order, and from strength to strength. You never learn how to manage a home by just existing. This is a kind of knowledge kept from you only until you buckle down and *do* it. This is knowledge that is gained *only* by experience, and lots of it.

In the early 1800s pastors used to write letters to their daughters before they married, telling them how to get ready, while they were still adolescents. They emphasized not depending upon their talents, or their good looks and high fashion, their drawing talent, their beautiful eyes, their agile waltzing, their lilting gorgeous singing voices, but to, instead, begin cultivating the ability to place a tasty bowl of soup in front of guests, to begin to keep the laundry steadily tidy, as a well formed habit, to know which garden tools to use to what purpose, and to begin a little financial log of money personally earned and spent?

These pastors stressed to their daughters that a man of high influence will have many domestic demands placed upon his future home with many guests and much hospitality called for continuously, and he will be carefully looking for a woman who has *management skills*, someone who could deftly take over that future home that he would entrust to her.

Seek to prepare your daughters to be fit to be First Ladies, to be able to run the domestic part of the White House, hosting dinners to receive world class dignitaries, and you'll begin to get the picture. They will really be in charge of much more than that for another better kingdom—even in their own ho-hum humble homes. You don't just wake up capable—you practice.

The public schools have failed miserably in this domestic charge. They taught young girls to dissect frogs for anatomy class (a skill they will never use again), but removed courses in home economics out of the schools, no longer teaching skills those girls will need every day of their lives. I have known of young mothers, so overwhelmed, so shaken with their domestic duties day in and day out, who have locked themselves in their bedrooms, cars, closets and let their children "hang from the chandeliers", they were so ill prepared. In our day and age, some men come home to houses filled with electronics, with no chairs. And some children dress themselves off of the floor.

Mothers, look at your daughters. When they mop up a spill on the floor, do they look and act confidently or do they function listlessly? When they approach dinnertime, do they look as if they've never seen one before? Where is the apron, the rolled up sleeves, the confident look in the eye? Begin today to take hold of yourself and your daughters and reverse this mediocrity that is plummeting countless American homes into chaos. Say no to outside activities and DVD's inside the home until you possess your home. *Really* possess it.

Garner a list of life principles

If we stay alert while we live, we'll begin to see that certain choices in life consistently yield better results. These wiser paths can be chosen in little practical matters as well as in larger relational matters. It is fun to make a growing list of these principles as you spot them. When a new occasion for the application of one emerges, you'll gain a certain confidence in life. You can say with repose, "Aha, here it is again, I'll proceed in this manner."

> "The path of the righteous grows brighter and brighter to the full day" (Proverbs 4:18).

Such a list could be handed down to your children and grandchildren, to spare them much needless hassle.

Here's an example of a wee practical one —

✓ Every time you need to mix ingredients in a pan or cook something on the stove, use a pan the next size larger than what you really need. You can mix and stir faster and get the job done quicker, without any spillage.

Example of a larger, relational one —

✓ Whenever you partner with someone in a business deal, write down, share and sign a description of your expectations and imagined conclusions. In every joint venture, even in the best of relationships, remember that the unspoken perceptions will, at times, be that each of you will think you are carrying the lion's share of the load and that the other person is doing nothing. Better yet, avoid such alliances all together. Go it alone. Scripture forbids financial partnerships with non-believers, because if the LORD has to judge the sin in the other person's life, your half of the venture will get swept into the fire, too (Amos 3:3; 2 Corinthians 6:14).

Here are others:

✓ If you don't finish going after the thing you started out to obtain, you lose all of your beginning energy.

✓ Washing dishes immediately (or at least, rinsing them) saves time, because nothing sticks. You may not even need soap.

✓ If you don't have enough time or money to do a project but you desperately want the results, simply **begin with what you have**. Often, a path will open before you, *as you go.* Consider the Biblical story of the loaves and the fish (Matthew 14).

Minimize the need to clean

Keep a lid on the making of messes on the front end.
Minimize your cleaning by reducing the need for it.

Examples:

1. Mat your house inside and out of all the entrances and exits. Less vacuuming.
2. Give each of your children one glass or cup to last all day. Assign a place for each cup and/or put a colored dot on it with a permanent marker, and teach each child what his color is. Less to wash.
3. Don't be laundering external clothes every day. The family can have clean, fresh underwear every day but wear pants, shirts, dresses and jumpers over and over. Change pillowcases every week but sheets every other week.

Life is more than laundry. Time saved here can be used for something more productive and lasting. It's a trade of needless maintenance for influence. By the way, the same principle holds true for the use of money. You can either swallow your dollars in fast food hamburgers that you'll never see again, or save much of that money for a hard good that lasts (a home and car), by eating at home.

Hands that work

In my experience, yellow latex housecleaning gloves are worthless. They tear on the way home. The green 15 mil flock lined chemical-resistant nitrile gloves, or the thick blue neoprene ones are the best. Buy good thick work gloves at a janitorial supply store or a hardware store. Choose one size larger than your hand size, so that you can slip them on and off effortlessly many times a day, plunging your hands in and out of all kinds of water, grime, grease, and sludge. Wearing these gloves dissolves all squeamishness over any unpleasant job. So "armed", there is no job that will defy you, no matter how dirty. Because you gain the upper "hand" physically, you gain it psychologically, too. Put 'em on, whistle Dixie, and go tackle your house.

Kitchen tips

How to hand-wash dishes better: Some women have washed dishes for nearly 60, 70, 80 years and still are "winging it" in their old age. How could we, as women, do something three times a day and know so little about it? Let's think it through *thoroughly* once and for all and get the best system down pat.

First, what's the attitude? Do you dread doing dishes? What can you *think* to make the whole relentlessly repetitive affair more tolerable? To begin with, to overcome inertia, think about the hot sudsy water, not the dirty dishes. Then lead with your hands: just begin doing it. Think about whether you *want* to do it or not *afterwards*—after it is all done. And then think about getting through the chore at record speed. You don't want to spend forever in the kitchen doing dishes. You want to do them *quickly* and get out of there.

Let's conquer doing the dishes by hand for those of you who don't have a dishwasher, and to mentally equip the rest of you for when you attend potlucks, or your dishwasher breaks, or you are at someone else's home who doesn't have one. You've got to know how to do dishes quickly and efficiently.

Ideally, you need two large plastic dishpans that fill your sink space: one for washing and one for rinsing. You want to use these plastic tubs, simply because you can go faster. You don't have to worry about chipping your sink or your dishes if they are surrounded with plastic. When your wash water gets dirty, empty it, then pour your rinse water from the other tub into your dish tub, add a little more dishwashing soap, and start all over. Refresh your water frequently. When you've finished, shake the excess water off of both your plastic tubs and fling them on top of your refrigerator to store them there to air dry. Save space under your sink for more important things. Set the top tub in perpendicular to the bottom one so they don't get stuck together.

You'll need four tools: a 12" bottle brush, an 8" scrubber brush with a tilted handle, a mild blue scrubber square (not a heavy-duty rough green one; those are rarely if ever needed), and a separate sponge. Because you want to be able to use both sides of your sponge to endlessly mop up counter top water in and around the sink, don't get the kind that has the scrubbie on the back side.

Primarily use the tilted handled brush to clean most every dish and pan, aided by your blue scrubbie square for harder spots, reserving your sponge for primarily wiping counter-tops and cleaning silverware. This keeps your sponge less gummed up and bacteria-laden from food particles. The brush is far easier to clean, and absorbs less long range crud.

Do not use dish rags. Only a small portion of a dish rag is used on a job, leaving a huge tail to drag around on your countertops and plates. It is the most inefficient of kitchen wannabees/inventions, and also is a huge germ trap. Keep them in the linen closet for use in the bathtub and shower.

First, dry-clean all your dishes by scraping them with a spatula into the trash. Toss all your dirty silverware into a flat-bottomed plastic shoebox-sized container. (Get one of these; you'll use it every day.) If you toss your silverware into a bowl, the bowl invariably tips over, spilling the heavy silverware all over the counter. If you toss the silverware onto a plate, it nearly always overruns the plate, falling off on all sides.

Wipe all grease with a tissue (far cheaper than a paper towel, and far less messy than coating all your other dishes in greasy water, as we discussed before).

You need three detergents: 1) non-toxic liquid dish soap, 2) white vinegar (never use white vinegar as food, but it makes a great cleaning agent to squirt in dirty pans; use apple cider vinegar to eat, but use white vinegar to soak stains and stubborn stuck-on food, to wipe mirrors and windows and to clean your iron), and 3) Borax (a non-toxic abrasive) for when needed (keep it available close by in a small dish or in a large-holed shaker).

If you are doing scores of pots and pans after a big Thanksgiving dinner, for example, spread a bath towel on your counter, take out your lower dishwasher drainer, and set it on the towel next to your little everyday dish drainer. This will provide ample extra room for a lot of things to air dry at once, allowing you to finish the overall job in half the time.

Take time to wash your blender/Vita-Mix™ and all pots and pans as soon as you empty the food out of them. If you have some food left over in the pan/blender, immediately empty it, too, into a jar or bowl so that you can plunge those big pieces into water right away. This produces far less work than scouring off all the stuck-on food later. Use the long tall brush to wash the blender, and use your little blue pad to scour the pans—and do it before you sit down to eat (wearing your rubber gloves).

Soak stubborn spots on the counter and stove top with soapy water dribbled over the spot with your sponge. Then go wash a few dishes, and then return to those soaked spots and quickly wipe them up; this eliminates all necessity for elbow grease. Since water is a solvent, let it do your work for you. Soak each little grouping of dishes, too, while you are rinsing the prior group which you have let stack up in the second sink. Soak, clean, rinse. Multitask. If company is coming at any minute, wash the *biggest* things first. If time is on your side, wash the *cleanest* things first. Done.

When your children do dishes, teach them to hustle, not dilly-dally. Set the timer; shave their time; give rewards. Listless children at work are a drain on the entire atmosphere. Let them relax later—not while doing a chore.

Coping with grease: Whenever you have to clean up a greasy pan, it gums up your pipes and lines your sink with an oily film. Also, if you have to debone any meat, you're all day trying to wash it off your hands, afterwards. You'll end both these problems, if you'll do two things.

One: Whenever deboning a turkey or chicken use those cheap, very thin, see-through vinyl surgical gloves. Purchase the latex-free 100-count package, so that you always have them "on hand!" Because you now aren't worried about the grease on your hands anymore, you can really attack that bird—salvaging every scrap. The money you save in gaining more meat will pay for the gloves. And, not surprisingly, you'll discover that you'll finish the job in half the time.

Two: Immediately, take the bird out of the pan and set aside to debone later, pour the grease out of the pan, into a see-through glass jar, using a spatula to get it all. Then use a tissue to wipe off both your spatula and bottom of your pan, before tossing your pan into your sudsy dishwater. Add one or two tablespoons of white vinegar to your water; let the pan soak while you go debone your bird. The vinegar will cut the tiny bit of grease that is left in your pan and help cut it off your sink and pipes as well. (By the way, wipe off your peanut butter knives with a tissue, too, before washing them. It will save the other dishes from a greasy film, save your pipes, and make your total dishwater less oily.)

Put your jar of meat juice/fat/grease into your refrigerator with a lid on it or saucer over it. Wait to have your gravy *tomorrow*. By that time, all the fat will have hardened to the top, which you now scrape off into the trash can, leaving perfectly greaseless, healthy yummy meat juice to use with your leftover meat as gravy or to use as soup stock. If you simply must have gravy on the first day that you cook your meat, use Imagine™'s Creamy Portobello Mushroom Soup™ for your gravy. This method of managing grease is a gift to your health and to your kitchen pipes.

Return to your pan—it will now be a pleasure to wash up.

If you want to eliminate dealing with grease all together, simply eliminate meat and dairy out of your diet. It may be doing to your insides what it is doing on your sink and hands. Watch the documentary movie, *Forks over Knives*.

Aprons and pie crusts

(1.) Make yourself the world's best apron.

If you want a better apron, this is an apron you can slosh dirty water on as you work at the kitchen sink. That means you can work fast and don't have to be so careful. And you can see your pretty clothes through it. Hang it on a hook in the kitchen where you can quickly grab it. You'll love this apron. I have several cloth aprons, but always grab this see-through vinyl one instead, whenever working in the kitchen.

Medium-weight clear plastic vinyl comes on 54-inch rolls in a department store's fabric department. Measure your favorite apron and go get some of that vinyl to match that measurement. Cut an apron out of it, attaching fabric only for a neck strap and waist ties out of fabric. When you sew the neck and waist ties to it, first cut a 2- by 2-inch scrap of vinyl and fold that over the apron's edges right at the spots where you'll attach the fabric, and stitch through all three layers of vinyl to really secure the ties.

(2.) Use your leftover vinyl scraps to make the tool for producing the world's best-looking pie crusts.
Out of your leftover scraps of this vinyl, cut two 13-inch circles to use for rolling out pie crusts. Draw around a plate; if your plate is only 12 inches in diameter, measure out an inch all around the edge, mark and cut.

Roll your pie crusts out between these two pieces of vinyl each and every time you make a pie, and your crusts will come out splendidly thin. Roll your dough to within 1/2 inch of the edge. Peel off the top layer of vinyl and plop the crust in your pie pan, then peel off the second layer, gently loosening it evenly all around the edges with your finger first. Your counter, hands and rolling pin all stay clean.

Pie crust recipe:
    2 C whole wheat flour
    1/4 C grapeseed oil (or any cooking oil)
    1/2 C rice milk or (other milk)

Mix in a small bowl. Stir with a metal dinner fork until the ball of dough chases your fork around the bowl. You'll think at first it is too wet, but keep stirring for a minute. You want your dough to be pliable, but not sticky. (If it is too sticky, add a touch more flour; if it is too stiff, add a touch more milk). But if you use the measurements above, it should come out just right. Let it sit for 10 minutes before rolling it out. This lets the flour thoroughly absorb the oil and milk, making it far easier to deal with.

Divide the dough in half. Roll out between your vinyl circles. Makes two. If dough spreads/rolls out beyond the edges tuck it back in between the layers, and re-finger-press it through the vinyl. Make it perfectly round at about 12.5".

Spiff up your spices

Artists have a palette full of beautiful colors to work from. For a cook, spices fulfill a similar purpose. Spices make your bland rice into exotic Indian cuisine. Indian and Chinese food tastes so good because they had to do *something* to make rice appealing to eat, yet *again*. Marco Polo went to China to gather rich spices; Columbus risked his life in search of them, too. Just because we have an abundance of them, don't forget what a gift from God they are. Their sheer variety is mind-boggling.   So, gather and organize your spices extremely well, once and for all.

For starters: throw out that flimsy whirligig-thing-a-ma-jig that you currently keep your spices on. Every time you give it a twirl, half your spices fall off. Two-thirds of your spices are hidden behind your front challengers and never even get used. And who *knows* where each spice *is*, in the first place, because they aren't alphabetized. Round and round we go, wasting time hunting, until we hang it up and don't use any spices, 'cause we couldn't find the right one, quick enough.

To end this kitchen time-waster, and repeated irritation, go to Home Depot or any lumber yard and purchase several 1" x 1" wooden sticks; they come in 4' lengths; redwood is nice. Have the gentleman in the lumber department cut them in foot long sections. Then come home and start stacking them in your shelves to make high risers like those used by choirs. Stack them from back to front, facing you. Stack five high in the back row, and three high in the next row forward, then use the shelf itself for your front row.   Then place your spices in alphabetical order upon these nice neat risers, perfectly sized to fit your spices. Just opening your cupboard will be an inspiration. You'll be able to grab each and every spice quickly and you'll look like a good cook— even if you aren't one yet.

Seven victory meals

Because every job has an infinite dimension to it, we gain mastery in this world only by narrowing our focus. If you'll pick out seven good "down-home dinners" that are suitable for serving to guests and prepare them over and over again, you'll end your cooking blues—*and* your feeling of incompetence. If you want to become super competent, try cooking these seven dinners week after week, steadily, for three months. Yup, the same things. This gives you 12 shots at making the same meal.

During these repetitions, purposely *improve*. Deliberately seek to shave your minutes and angle for ways to multitask. Write down each of your seven meals in a notebook, one per page, and then continue to write *all over that thing* each time you prepare it. Function from your notebook. Which thing did you do first? What could you have done better? While you are sautéing one thing, you are chopping another, or quickly washing the pan from the thing before. Write down your improvements, either because you just did them and they worked our great, or because you want to try a different method, or sequence, next time.

> **Your goal?** To be able to prepare this meal effortlessly, in record time, on the backstroke, mindlessly, while conversing with dinner guests.

Make your seven-day plan around the meals you already do somewhat well, or if you feel bone dry, with no ideas at all, if you are a meat eater, try arranging your dinners largely around those meats: chili, meat loaf, salmon, chicken, roast, spaghetti, and popcorn and apples (for your final, easy day).

If money is tight and/or you are eating vegan these days for health reasons, do it with starches/beans/grains/soups: pinto bean soup, wild rice salad meal, split pea soup, black beans, lentil soup, corn soup, vegetable soup. To stretch your grocery money let the weekly grocery store loss-leader sales guide you in making your menu plans.

(If you are striving to eat mostly raw, you still need to know how to prepare these aforementioned types of meals for others who don't eat raw—to have conquered them in detail, in advance.)

The reason we don't gain confidence in the kitchen is because we endlessly change plans. (Translation: fly by the seat of our pants, night after night.) Try this 7X12 strategy and you'll be an expert in three months, the envy of the entire neighborhood, and all your relatives. If you don't try it, you'll still be three months older—either with the expertise or without it. You don't want to wind up a 90 year old and still not know the exact number of minutes it takes to boil a soft-boiled egg at your altitude and have it come out just right. It can happen to all of us. Just keep changin' plans.

Small canning jars for multi-purpose storage

We've all heard of the large Ball™ canning jars. But have you discovered the inexpensive little 8-ounce ones? If you do get a case of them, be sure to buy the easy white **plastic** lids next to them, to go with them—and use those lids instead of the metal ones with the rings when storing dried goods. Then you can buy your major spices in bulk. I use these little jars, arranged neatly in a row and labeled for parsley, cilantro, chili, curry, all purpose seasoning, and dried teas. You can also use them to store extra juice or coconut milk in the fridge, and for little treats or liquids (use the tighter sealing metal rings for liquids) when running errands to town (they'll fit neatly and snugly in your purse), as well as in your hubby's lunch box.

Home management objective #8:
Extend hospitality

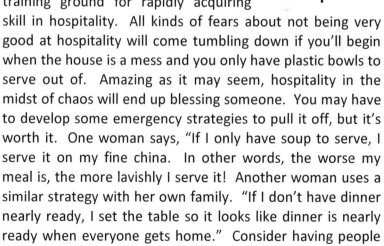

Hospitality is never convenient. The best way to learn to do it is by *doing* it. A sort of baptism by fire is the best training ground for rapidly acquiring skill in hospitality. All kinds of fears about not being very good at hospitality will come tumbling down if you'll begin when the house is a mess and you only have plastic bowls to serve out of. Amazing as it may seem, hospitality in the midst of chaos will end up blessing someone. You may have to develop some emergency strategies to pull it off, but it's worth it. One woman says, "If I only have soup to serve, I serve it on my fine china. In other words, the worse my meal is, the more lavishly I serve it! Another woman uses a similar strategy with her own family. "If I don't have dinner nearly ready, I set the table so it looks like dinner is nearly ready when everyone gets home." Consider having people over for breakfast or lunch; it's easier and cheaper to fix than dinner.

Fast-action hospitality priorities: When you have to flip into hospitality mode, it works best to have a set of priorities well thought through ahead of time that you'll work from. When your family brings home guests home unannounced, or they arrive on their own, unannounced, if it is possible, have your children or husband answer the door or entertain them for a few minutes, while you quickly go groom yourself.

This may involve rapidly changing into a nicer dress, taking a fast glance in the mirror to make sure your hair is neatly pinned, barretted or tied back and doesn't present a wild, frenzied picture. Bare your teeth in front of the mirror, too, to double check if they look clean. And then swiftly run a damp paper towel around the bathroom sink and seat of the toilet in the bathroom that your guests are most likely to use. The reason it is important to groom yourself and prepare their bathroom first, is that you won't get a chance to do these things after your guests arrive. You can always set the table and chop veggies while talking with your guests, but the presentation of a harried, unkempt you and a repulsive bathroom are the first two interfaces with your home. You want them both to be as pleasant as possible. If it is not possible to attend to both of these things, then make up for these lacks by an extra sparkle in your smile and eye. Show extra interest in your guests and extra charm in the way you interact with them. They'll be so blessed, they won't notice anything else.

Set the stage for hospitality: To be hospitably-minded means you will think through how to serve people in detail, before such an occasion arises. Carefully conquer the details of how you'll serve both a meal and offer a bed.

Always have a meal in the cupboard that requires no time to cook. With canned or dehydrated food you can open the cans or add water and instantly serve something. Even rice cakes, almond butter and tea are counted as welcome by someone in trouble. People need *you*; what food you serve is secondary. This one aspect of hospitality (food preparation), is so overwhelming to most women that it dive-bombs oceans of hospitality. Conquer it and move off of dead center. For all occasions you can rapidly put a pot of rice on the stove and be 90% done. Go greet your guests and return to add something to it later. Try steaming frozen veggies (eliminates cleaning, and cutting) and add curry, cashews, raisins and coconut. Finished! Stock whatever ingredients you'll need for your unforseen hospitality dinner needs, all the time.

To be truly hospitable, check your guest room for the following specific items: a spare brand new toothbrush, a small alarm clock, facial tissues, pencil and paper, small trash can, a good devotional book, closet hangers or hooks in the wall and space in closet, enough empty surface area to lay out a suitcase comfortably, individual towel rods fastened to the wall next to their bed (or a portable towel rack), a flashlight for navigating around your unfamiliar home in the middle of the night,

a small snack (fruit bars, bottle of juice and purified water, etc.), towel and wash rag, tiny bottles of shampoo/ deodorant/ soap, a large terry cloth bathrobe laid across the bed, cleanser and scrubber obviously available and ready to use near the tub and sink, and plastic gloves. It's also nice to include a full-length mirror within the bedroom, several pillows to choose from, and extra blankets. And, a small electric heater, a good reading lamp located next to bed or chair, a little box of safety pins, scissors, adhesive tape, aspirin, etc. And for the bathroom, small tiny paper drinking cups and matches (if a guest wants to deodorize the bathroom after each use).

If you outfit one bedroom and one bathroom ahead of time with such detailed, thoughtful things, the message of love and real care for a person in time of need will be loud and clear. They will feel utterly cherished. You will be ministering hospitality by emotional warmth *and* by substance.

Well-ordered hospitality: Sophisticated hospitality is summed up in two words: advance preparation. Have every detail fully prepared the day ahead, and you'll still find additional details that crop up on the actual day. Build artificial heat to make yourself get fully ready far ahead of schedule. Do not choose kinds of food that must be prepared, cut up, glazed, and steamed at the last minute. Remind yourself that your guests will eat loads of other meals at other times when they can prepare last-minute delicacies themselves. The goal is to feed them, not to restore their entire health for them or to serve them the freshest food that ever crossed a set of teeth.

Set the table, iron the tablecloth, choose the music, lay out your outfit, cook and make all the food ahead of time, clean up all the cooking pots, etc. On the day, just warm and serve.

Set limits for your hospitality: Before you get into a long-range hospitality situation, set limits based on your own capacity. Remember Ben Franklin's statement: "Fish and visitors stink after three days." You can always add days, but you will find it most embarrassing to have to ask your guests to leave if they over-stay. Three days is a good amount of time to enjoy the upside of one another, after which it is only human nature to begin to compare, criticize and want to reform one another. If their stay will be for more than three days, set a limit on how much you'll cook. "I'll prepare every evening meal but you are on your own for breakfast and lunch" (offering your fridge and cupboards if you desire). Or if their stay is even lengthier, you can offer half of your fridge (or one shelf) and half the dining room table for them to prepare their own meals. If you'll set such limits up front, you'll avoid embarrassments later. You may find relating to one family at a time rather than several families minimizes misunderstandings and the stresses of several sets of differing expectations, personality conflicts, etc., and maximizes your chances for relating at deeper, more consequential levels.

> The essence of hospitality is to welcome others into your heart. The hospitable woman trades "Here I am" for "There you are!"

Home management objective #9:
Raise the relational bar

If you don't have a strong relational life
with your core relationships (i.e., spouse
and children), you're dead in the water.
Let other relationships suffer, if need be, but not these, if
you want spiritual strength in your life.

We all know how to relate at home when things are going
well. It's when things go south that we have a hard time.
Perhaps it's impossible to avoid all of a family's relational
colliding, no matter how careful you are in avoiding potential land mines. Because we are all human and have a dark
side, we'll all encounter tough relational patches. However,
as Christians each of us is a new man as well as an old man
(2 Corinthians 5:17, Galatians 6:15). The fray can get exceptionally messy in an hour when all of our "old men" bump
into one another, simultaneously. It's what we do in our
thought lives as the new man afterwards that matters.
That's why David said, "May the words of my mouth *and the
meditations of my heart* be acceptable unto you, oh LORD"
(Psalm 19:14). To think thoughts after God, to sandwich
ourselves down between His thoughts—immediately after
we catch ourselves having had our own ugly thoughts, is
where we need to learn to run habitually.

In your thought life, *make* those meditations of your heart
be right. Moment by moment, fix them, mend them, build
them, and patch them until they hold up under the Heavenly
Father's scrutiny. The most powerful way to arrest wayward
meditations is to lasso them with Scripture. Say a Scripture.
Have several handy.

We must leave no dark thought unchallenged by the good. Let's examine how to apply such strategies with our husbands and then with our children.

With your husband: First: pray for him. He may have a headache, a hidden anxiety, or a knee-jerk response from his own childhood. Prayer will immediately change him from your bitter enemy (at the moment) to your needy brother within your own mind. Second: look at the situation from *his* point of view. Wholesome perspective and renewed love for your spouse will stumble all over themselves to set you on the right path again. If there is a moment when your husband has been harsh, cranky, critical, or impatient, Satan may fling a thought into your mind, "Some other man may be better." If such an ungodly thought should come, counter it by doing some extra little thing immediately to love your husband. You'll find that deadly thought will stick its tail between its legs and scamper away. It missed its mark; instead it made you love your husband more.

If your husband becomes totally irksome and unreasonable, say to yourself, "Well, someone has got to love him, or he'll be alone in the world because he'll drive everyone from himself!" You can deliberately operate in the opposite spirit and say to yourself, "In me he shall find a place of a thousand forgivings and constant love. It is my job. It is my joy!"

Take his contrariness as an exciting challenge to marshal your love around him yet another time. Learn to view his off moments as "character-growth-boot-camp" for you.

A woman's flexibility, ingenuity and intuition are gifts given by God for just such a purpose.

Make it a habit to submit now, discuss later. You don't need to take everything to the mat. Let lots of little irritations go. Consequential conflicts can be let go until a more desirable time for talking presents itself. But try to talk soon afterwards, keeping short accounts. Good non-threatening communication keeps love flowing between you.

If your husband shirks certain duties in one area or another, saddle up next to him and actually help him finish the task. He may just be paralyzed by the thought of it and needs a buddy. Encourage and motivate him for next time by showing him how freeing it is to stay on top of necessary paperwork or maintenance.

You are not ultimately responsible for your husband's choices. You are responsible to work on *you*. And pray for him. The more you try to fulfill your own role well, the less you'll be bothered by your spouse not filling his.

If you are prone to anger, learn how to wrench your thoughts away from the present exasperating moment and fixate on a totally different idea, a pleasant project you're working on, a pleasant person you know, or a piece of beauty you like to see. The moment will pass, you'll have no regrets, and you can take up discussion of it at a time that is less volatile for both of you. Train yourself to immediately look to Jesus when you're about to lose it. He'll totally calm you down. It's a mystery; it's a miracle on command, at your disposal, at any time, anywhere. Use it. "A fool gives full vent to his anger, but a wise man keeps himself under control" (Proverbs 29:11).

Be swift to forgive. As one Christian martyr wrote, "Don't waste your vital strength on unforgiveness toward your torturer." Get over it—and get on with it.

With your children: Remember, there is a payday coming. Certain interchanges with you will fix themselves like huge printing in the sky of their memories, to be re-lived again and again in their adult years, from *their* perspectives. Again, look at your family life from your children's point of view as you live it.

When they are little, firmness is needed (as we discussed already in Part 2 about child training.) In general, focus on "landing" each deviant behavior with consequences that are counterproductive to their own self-interest. Make them see that their bad behavior costs *them*, not you.

But when they reach adolescence there needs to be more communication of your motives and of the intents behind your parenting. More space needs to be given for the emerging personality. Remain firm in requiring kindness, but think of ways to serve your adult children, too: to welcome them home from activities; to provide a cheerful warm home that they love to return to.

Be very, very mindful that you are creating lifetime memories for them—memories that loom larger than any subsequent imprinting ever will. You are either fixing in their hearts a desire to be with you or a compulsion to avoid you if you remain too controlling. If you have done your job well in early childhood (of instilling their responsibility to God), you should be able to gradually ease yourself out of the job—moving from "sage on the stage" to "guide on the side." Listen to them a lot. Be there for them. If you retain a controlling spirit you may win the battle (get your temporary desired behavior out of them) but lose some of their "want to", later. Start with law and end with grace. Many parents have it backwards. They are too loose when their children are young, and too tight when they're mature. **Treat your children as if you won't have them next year. But *train* them as if they won't have *you*.**

With others: If you are prone to compare yourself with others, realize that it's unproductive. "For we dare not class ourselves or compare ourselves. They who compare themselves among themselves, are not wise" (2 Corinthians 10:12, NKJV). The more you try to be like others, the more you'll always be a second-best "them". In contrast, the more you follow Christ, the more unique you'll become. Recognize that junior high peer pressure squeezed many of us into many shallow cultural social should's and ought's, not found in the Bible, that we then have to spend the rest of our life shedding.

Home management objective #10:
Hone your homeschooling

In Deuteronomy chapters 4 through 6 we see that the Biblical model is for you to educate your own children at home. Here are some thoughts for finessing how to do that.

Are you sure you have the right curriculum?

We've observed a troublesome academic pattern after spending two decades in the homeschool movement, heavily involved on the front lines at state conventions. We find that many parents are able to competently and tenaciously train the brains of their children for short durations. But soon burnout follows. The single biggest cause of homeschooling burnout is choosing the wrong curriculum. For this reason, we recommend obtaining a through, sequential curriculum for your child and then you can waltz on and off his "page" as you have energy and passion to teach him those specific additional academics that really matter to you, (if you are sure that they have not already been covered somewhere else in the curriculum).

For most homeschoolers, veterans and beginners alike, the illusion is that you will always have *perfect* days in which to teach, but the reality is that you'll seldom have even one perfect homeschooling day. If your schooling centers on you as the teacher, it will simply slip through the cracks on days when other demands take over. Because schooling is the one flexible/negotiable part of the day (no one is watching), it often gets put on the back burner (for far too many days, for months on end), because today we can't do it *right*, using what you *thought* was the ideal curriculum.

Too often, moms—because they have never been down this path before (they graduated from nursing school, or business school, or...)—inadvertently choose and purchase curriculums that are heavily mother-dependent. They purchase curriculum based on topics that they wish they had had in school, or books that look fabulous, or techniques that seem new and innovative and far superior to the way *they* were taught.

However, **the problem is not the content or style of the program, at all, but rather it is one of administration.** Is this curriculum easy to administer? Can your children do it without you? Ask yourself: Is it going to be easy to get through each day with this curriculum, especially when I am preoccupied with little Johnny who just threw up, or I'm on an emergency phone call, or we have unexpected company? Then what happens? What happens when I'm up all night with another child and have to sleep IN in the morning? Let's see...hmm...five children times two "mom-isn't-available-to-teach" hours per student equals 10 wasted hours for the family that morning. We have seen children who are now the grown products of this little daily nightmare, and it isn't pretty.

Unit studies

In far too many cases, these idealistic theories about curriculum have been murdered by a few brutal facts—embarrassing facts. The children didn't get thoroughly educated—not even as much as *we* were educated in inferior secular schools. Scores of excited moms who have never taught a child through all 12 grade levels tell me sentences like this: "This fall we are going to study George Washington—in fact, we'll do a unit study on him!" The problem is that the mom doesn't see the 12-year big picture that there are over

34,000 concepts to cover to even make your child *aware* of the most rudimentary components of the big wide world out there.   Giving three months to one concept won't cut it.   While mom is fixated on her one euphoric idea of what she will teach, time is wasting.   Sand literally pours through the hourglass of childhood.   What she is not aware of is that children can learn 10 times faster than she can even dream up the topics, let alone provide a newly hunted down perfect book to teach it with.

Moms with extra time? Go ahead and buy all of the super-idealized curriculum you want.   But this year try teaching it in the evenings or on the weekends when you get that one "supercharged-mommy-moment" a week, but for all the remainder of the time, for all those "barely-making-it" hours, get a curriculum that your children can do without you.   Waltz onto their page on any day at any time that you want to teach them from your own academic passions—we always teach our passions best—but for all the other days, and the other hours, keep your children's noses to the grindstone of an established curriculum that gets the job done without you.

Ask yourself a question: How much extra time did I have yesterday to write out lesson plans, or to thumb through a textbook to figure out what my child should be doing today?   Was it three minutes? 30 seconds? Oops, just couldn't get to it? Then what makes you think you'll have that time tomorrow? If you must read a teacher's edition to figure out what your child should do, you are already sunk before you start.   Get a program that doesn't tie you to a teacher's manual.   If your children can't just proceed in an obvious manner out of their own books, the program is too complicated.

All the "not-so-hot" choices out there

Some love those big companies that sell you the huge **textbook for every subject**, that look like the public school's texts. But quickly you'll find that the sheer size of the books scares children off before they even open the covers. In addition that thick size is cumbersome to haul around on errands when you are trying to use small moments wisely. And parents by the scores have already discovered that these programs can be tedious "drill and kill and over-kill" curriculums, despite the expensive packaging. They cost too much, weigh too much, take too much preparation out of your hide, and bore your children to tears with excessive unnecessary mental labor.

Then there are the super dense **spiritual curriculums**. Everyone in the family reads this and that and does this project and that project on one character trait, together. Fine. Purchase those and teach one every Sabbath, or work through one for one evening a week to gather as an entire family to study. But for two to six hours a day every day of the week, they require too much of mama—and too much of everyone else. On most days, one can't even find the whole family to study with, let alone *do* it. If you use one of these programs, you'll burn out, guaranteed.

Then there is the **eclectic approach**: using one supposedly top-notch book for this and one "top-notch" book for that. I hope you like shopping more than teaching—because your children will read them and finish them on the way to the car. You'll have to turn right around and spend the next week locating another one.

Some parents pick books that they themselves like over topics they missed, initially wanting to study along with their children. But upon a closer reflection, the parent already went through 12 years of school; it is not necessary to be made to do it all over again, at this time. One *can* study after one's children grow up and leave home. The question becomes this: do you want to have a life along with schooling, or do you want academics to rule your life and home? (Our item #67 on *Two Most Common Pitfalls* also describes the dangers of falling into academic idolatry.)

Then there is the **hands-on**, build-everything-you-read-about, pyramids-under-the-kitchen-table approach. This approach absorbs far too much time spent on "pyramids" (single subjects)—which a child can readily understand just by looking at a few pictures—to the exclusion of time that could have been spent on other equally important concepts or subjects. Life isn't just endless time on your hands. Time spent under the table is time lost practicing a new scale on an instrument.

Then there is the "**read-every-book-in-sight**" curriculum. Just read. Tons of homeschooling families pride themselves on what good readers their children have become. These parents mistakenly think that makes their children exempt from producing anything mental. Most all homeschooling families produce good readers. This is commonplace, with few exceptions. Parents can't see that this is not unusual, because they only see inside their own house. Reading is just not the whole picture. What if your car only had a motor, no steering wheel, no brakes, and no seats? Math is important, writing is important, physics is important, spelling is important, each of them requiring very little reading and a great deal of doing. The first time your child hears about atoms and molecules and has only read history books, he is apt to say "Huh?" or worse yet, start feeling the "Huh?" going on inside himself everywhere he turns. A general education requires gaining basic familiarity with thousands of diverse concepts.

What about unschooling?

A reader sent us a devastating article by Kate Hammer, education reporter for *The Globe and Mail*, entitled "The Deschooling and Unschooling Movement Is Growing." The writer's misguided joy is a sad commentary on our culture. Her article begins thus: "A small but growing movement known as deschooling, life learning, unschooling, and edupunk is home-schooling returned to its postwar progressive roots, far from the Bible-thumping mould that has come to dominate the modern image of home-schoolers." Kate continues, "Unschooling takes children out of schools, but, unlike a lot of home-school approaches, it doesn't import the classroom into the home. It does away altogether with educational clutter such as curricula and grades. Unschoolers maintain that a child's learning should be curiosity-driven rather than dictated by teachers and textbooks, and that forcing children to adhere to curricula quashes their natural inclination to explore and ask questions." The reader asked if we have an opinion on this trend. As one who student-taught in such an "open classroom" in the early 1970s, I experienced this unschooling experiment/disaster firsthand.

Here's what I wrote the person who sent this article to us, asking our opinion.

Yes, I have an opinion about unschooling: proponents of this theory ought to be run out of town—for the damage they do to the next generation. This theory has been around since the Garden of Eden. Basically, it is academic lawlessness. In the 1960s-1980s I saw an entire generation fall through the cracks, as products of their *educated* parents' experimentation. The children paid the price of aimless years, growing in nothing but indulged willfulness.

The school districts that adopted these theories for their classrooms paid for it dearly in their results. In the decades that followed, they let in academic chaos, all the way from kindergarten to the universities. The "new math" was so "out there", no one could use it in the real world. It was abandoned years later. The "no–phonics, only-sight-words" approach left the child dependent upon those limited sight words, and utterly lost when they encountered any reading beyond the basics. Phys Ed instructors allowed children to lie all over the gym floor throwing temper tantrums, together, as part of their accepted, enlightened curriculum, because it got it out of their systems in a "controlled way" and worked their lungs—rather than to acquire better skill aiming a ball. Similarly, graffiti boards were placed in the school bathrooms so that disgruntled children could "safely" write all over the walls—that is, until the first words to appear "reamed out" the very administrators and principals who had so "wisely" put them there.

Universities are accommodating English classes in pornography. Further, multiculturalism has elbowed its way into the universities, increasingly shifting the curriculum toward countless minority concerns rather than skill development. Multiculturalism is, in effect, the practice of acquiescing to every newly arriving group's cultural and language minutiae, rather than requiring the newbies to fit in with what is already here. Should our national language (and all school instruction) be equally English, Spanish, Italian, Chinese, Japanese, Mandarin, Swahili AND Arabic? Where does it stop? The melting pot is not what we have today. We now have separate cultures that are becoming ever more militant toward each other, while also taking more and more ground in both schools and government to rule by intimidation.

If you throw out curriculum and choose not to acquire the basics of a general education, coursework becomes any mini-culture's, hippie's, interest group's or union's immediate whim—and increasingly accommodates any fringe or deviant behavior.

Even within the current Biblically-based homeschooling movement, we have seen the results of children who have been raised under this theory of being led by curiosities, and they are very sorry adults—taking low-end jobs and playing video games. Most anything they write or say is loaded with mistakes, and they don't know how to *think* beyond going to the counter to purchase a candy bar.

The public school system *was* awful, but homeschooling solved two of its biggest problems: lots of one-on-one careful tutoring via parental attention, and two: no labeling/comparisons/and peer pressures. These produced outstanding results for the past several decades. To take it further and throw out the content (line upon line acquisition of mental skill, sequentially gained) is a disease of modern thinking.

This mental lawlessness has invaded all of modern thought. A woman's body now is no indication of meaning (enroll her for hand to hand combat in the military; give her a pill to get rid of the bother of having children). Language is no indication of meaning ("the author didn't really mean this or that; it means what *you* want it to"). Drinking and robbery are a disease. The people who engage in either are not held responsible/accountable for his/her actions. Currency doesn't need to be backed by gold; instead, it is the instrument of derivatives that no one will ever require you to pay—you just pass the leverage on down the line. And on and on it goes. Unschooling is basically anything goes; it is godlessness.

There is a *reason* why European royalty acquired tutors for their children from infancy onward and pulled them out of any public education. To be unschooled? Hardly! The purpose was to train those future kings and queens more rigorously—not to have them sit at home and stare at the walls and wait for their curiosities to shift. Nearly all of our U.S. Presidents have done the same with their own children. Watch what presidents/politicians *do*, not what they say. Regardless of how much they claim to support state education, they hire expensive tutors for their own children and send them to exclusive private schools. There is a *reason* why Asians, Europeans, Israelis, etc., have come to America for decades: because our educational institutions used to have academic standards. Immigrants clearly wanted the greatest academic edge they could find on the planet. But currently the modern university is in a state of meltdown and this sort of excellence is no longer true for the humanities departments, although many engineering, science and math programs still have some semblance of classical training/tradition left.

There is a *reason* why the forefathers of our country, many of them homeschooled, were able to frame a constitution that didn't fall apart for 200 years. Because they were so well educated, their thinking was seasoned and mature. They understood how to limit the evils of history because they had studied history—as well as the ordered grammar with which to write the document. And there is a *reason* why so many high-achieving Asian parents start their children on musical instruments and science when they are three, building superior skill through disciplined, line upon line development.

Because a parent trains their child sequentially in the morning doesn't mean they shut down their curiosities for the remainder of the day. The two are by no means exclusive, as unschoolers claim. Look at the Biblical injunction in Deuteronomy 6:7: train them in the basics first, while you are walking and talking. Historically, Jewish boys have memorized the Torah by age 13; *then* they were ready to ask questions about it as adolescents. The questions then stemmed from a developed curiosity, with a language to express it and some facts to fling around. To fling around "hot air" gets nobody anywhere. This truly emanates from the Pit—and our culture is saturated with it. In every area of life, if you let go of absolutes and disciplined cores, chaos is the guaranteed result. There will be an academic debt to pay. As a culture in decline, we are swimming in it, as we speak.

A curriculum for the long ride

You can't see the full extent of it now, but teaching your children for 12 years is a long ride. You're going to be trotting around this homeschool barn several hours a day with several children for many years. Therefore, you need to have a dependable horse to ride—unless you want a circus at your house every day because you didn't spend enough time last night prepping for some other scenario.

Keep in mind that if you are a conscientious parent you *can* teach your child with any curriculum or most any book. All through history it has been done in scores of differing ways. Remember that there are materials available today that didn't even exist 100 years ago, but still people got educated. The curriculum choices are all yours, and yours alone to make. But if you want some help navigating through the curriculum jungle, here's our advice. We made this choice after seeing many moms in tears at conventions, year after year, who had made a whale of a lot of false starts. If you want this info, read on. If not, skip this section. (The next section is: Beyond Curriculum: Managing the Mental Diet of Your Child.)

When reading through this, keep in mind that you can pick and choose pieces from countless other good curriculums and resources to add to this basic plan—*if* you have the extra energy. That extra energy may grow thinner and thinner through the years.

The most important reason we picked this particular program over all other curriculums is that the child immediately learns how to carry the responsibility for his own education.

The curriculum is called ACE. It stands for Accelerated Christian Education. Other curriculums demand that parents spend preparation time in lesson planning and correcting. In ACE this time-consuming unnecessary taskmaster is eliminated for the parent who also has to do the laundry, fix dinner, etc. ACE is a simply administered program.

Even if your child is only exposed to ACE's sequential, consecutive, line upon line, precept upon precept material and hypothetically never fills in a single blank, or merely answers the questions aloud, or even just hears the paces read to him by an older sibling, (when he is not up to it, on sick days, for example) and keeps no records, and isn't multi-sensing every concept—he will *still* be light-years ahead of the child who hasn't. He will have at least encountered all of these thousands of concepts. Four pace booklets a day, four concepts per booklet, five days a week, 36 weeks a year, for 12 years, yields 34,560 concepts. Ta-dah!!!! Did you catch that? This is all done *for* you. You didn't have to even get out of your easy chair. This year, try teaching whatever else you want *on top of that*—but not in place of it. Countless very burned out families have switched to ACE after trying everything else they had in mind, and the smiles have returned. There have been no regrets.

We recommend ACE[6] for 12 reasons:

1. ACE is taught using thin booklets. It is easier to go to town and back with the thin ACE PACEs (work booklets—and actually *use* them on the trip) than to cart around large textbooks

---

[6] Accelerated Christian Education Customer Service: PO Box 299000, Lewisville, Texas 75029-9000; phone 1-800-925-7777 to order; website www.ACEMinistries.com ; email CustomerService@ACEministries.com

which the student may not even open, due to their bulkiness—and his dread. Most of us didn't like workbooks of any size when growing up because they were godless. Godless education is boring. Not so with these little gems. They have a totally different "feel" to them.

2. ACE is comprehensive. Nothing will fall through the cracks. It is academically sequential and rigorous. Graduates consistently score well on standardized tests and college entrance exams.

3. ACE is spiritual: you won't produce an intelligent graduate who has no morals. ACE is truly Biblical. The child is brought again and again to think upon God through its pages, and all of its concepts. Biblical thinking is not merely tacked on at the beginning or end. Children end up loving God through the study of their homeschool subjects.

4. ACE is engaging and uplifting, and keeps their interest, both academically and spiritually. It is both well-written and colorfully displayed. The pages look inviting.

5. ACE is self-taught. It is not mommy-dependent, and therefore it actually happens every day, regardless of the other sorts of chaos mom may be embroiled in at the moment.

6. ACE is self-corrected; the student has instant feedback. If you want to grade all your children's work, go ahead, have at it. But they won't grow if you do their evaluation. Weeks' worth of stacked papers that mom will someday get around to grading trains your child in absolutely nothing. When your children receive back all of your delayed grading with your meticulous and conscientious red marks, they will mindlessly throw those same papers into the trash. Sound familiar? If they grade their own as soon as they finish each pace, they will be invested in it themselves, to their own surprise. It is that simple. Correcting one's work is where all the growth takes place. Do you really have this much extra time? Would you not rather read a good book or take a walk with your child?

7. ACE is the curriculum for tear reduction. Momma doesn't burn out. She actually likes her children *and* gets dinner on the table—and wants to continue homeschooling next year.

8. ACE is priced at the low end of curriculums; you don't have to rob a bank or incur debt to buy it. The entire year costs less than one month's tuition at a private Christian school. It is so inexpensive, grandparents may be able to help you purchase it if finances are tight. You won't grow bitter halfway through the year because you sank two grand into a curriculum that you now hate but can't possibly switch out of, because you mortgaged the house to get it.

9. ACE trains outstanding character, woven into the full page text of every subject—as well as adds inserts of extra "wisdom pages". Character training is not tacked on as a token at the end of the entire day just to make the curriculum *look* spiritual.

10. Employers love to hire ACE graduates for any type of work, because they have found year after year that these students' cheerful work-ethic is second to none.

11. ACE is in 135 countries and currently educates well over three million children. It is tried and true. Children actually graduate; they actually score high on standardized tests; they actually get scholarships at colleges.

12. ACE is guilt free, because school actually gets done.

ACE is a good basic horse to ride. In the evenings you can grow your children even further through enrichment reading. Your children can voraciously read history, biography and how-to books without limit. And in the afternoons and on weekends you can further train them in domestic skills. Teach them how to earn and save a dollar. Turn off the TV and videos and curb the endless "goes nowhere" recreational fantasy reading, and you'll produce super children. This strategy of using ACE day in and day out, while adding occasional teaching from your own passions, and other materials will end the oscillating between valiant weeks and breakdown weeks that presently plague far too many home-schooling homes.

If you *do* use ACE, remember to stay flexible. If there is something you would like to have your child learn *sometime*, and it is happening now, spontaneously let it happen. Don't interrupt the momentum of it just because it wasn't sched-uled. (Incidentally, one of the best times to teach your children is while they are eating. They eat all the time, so that should give you plenty of time.) For ideas on optimal daily scheduling, order our homeschooling to-do charts booklet/Kindle book #105; it will help you get on track and stay on track with sure success.

Beyond curriculum: managing the mental diet of your child

Your child's brain is sacred ground. What gets written on his brain is largely your responsibility for about 12 years running, and cannot ever be erased once it is in there. In the beginning, he is like a new sponge: soft and supple and absorbent. He will sponge up grimy water or pristine mountain spring water—depending upon where you set him. Sponging up endless media can sadly damage a child in some hidden ways not experienced by children born in other centuries.

Sitting in front of hours and hours of entertainment has be-come a substitute for real life in many homes today, includ-ing Christian ones. Internet surfing and watching movies and TV rob a childhood of developmental hours spent in skill acquisition, self-initiative, relational interchanges, and high productivity. In many cases, entertainment has replaced the wholesome work ethic—even any appetite for it, as the body is repeatedly and ongoingly lulled into passivity.

If you entertain a child too often, you rob him of the ability to think UP an activity by himself and for himself. Staring at the baseboards has value, for a toddler, because eventually a child casts around to *do* something other than stare at the baseboards—but you have to withdraw the entertainment long enough to birth the initiation. Sitting in the great outdoors will birth even more initiation. Children who are sitting in front of dizzying frenetic advertisements indoors day after day do not grow the ability to have a consecutive reflective thought.

As a child, Edison would have been robbed of his tinkering time, the Wright Brothers of their daydreams while they were lying on their backs, staring at the sky. To constantly watch someone *else* live life robs you of *yours*. And to be stirred up about someone else's football game/score, or someone else's emotional trauma/dilemma in a TV story diverts the developing child from his own high intrigue. Hours get robbed from developing his own home based business that grows an unbelievable personal confidence, or cultivation of his own talent that brings untold beauty and pleasure to others, if done well—i.e. through mega hours of practice. And there is certainly no time to tend to or alleviate someone's real suffering down the street. There's no time—period. It has all been given over, sold out, and is unavailable.

Instead of parking your child in front of a screen, let him listen to adult conversations. Have him simply be with you, next to you, within earshot of you, at your same dinner table with the guests. The child will soon learn how to shape an interesting conversation, how to respond lovingly, and how to stick with a person emotionally. All of this mature (instead of peer based) social exposure will help him mature at an astonishing rate. Also, he will have enough reflection time to begin to learn how to think progressively—i.e., reach a conclusion—something denied the chronic dissipated TV watcher. Some children don't even know where the OFF button to their TV is located. It has been on since they were born.

And finally the other real fear, for a conscientious parent, *should* be the altered realities that children are escorted into via the screen—where evil is called good and good evil, where children dip down into fantasy worlds whose principles are in direct conflict with Scripture. They encounter creatures and activities that are nowhere found in reality, which give rise to fears, paranoia, anxieties and bad dreams that children were never meant to have.

These parallel realities are in the same camp with divination and witchcraft, and in fact may have been formed there. In the old days, children read stories about things that could happen in their own life with their own dog. Something different is going on today. Modern movies are invitations into parallel realities. Children are escorted there swiftly through overpowering visuals and pounding, driving action. The addiction is life-altering at profound levels not understood immediately. As busy, over-extended parents, all we knew was that we "needed" the convenience of the visual babysitter. But our *need* has become *their* addiction.

Even Christian films may have problems, not the least of which is dragging a child's formative brain through the cartoon or buffoon renderings of Biblical characters and even of God Himself which then, ever after, relentlessly come to his mind each and every time he wants to pray. Hours and hours of Christian movies straddle our children with having to go through a thickly layered visual interface to get to the real deal, the real spiritual realm. It is no gift.

The ideal plan would be to allow no exposure to TV, movies or Internet until a child is a 10-year-old (when he has the ability to distinguish between the abstract and the concrete)—and even after that, to limit it. Let the child have a fighting chance to have a real childhood, unmolested by visual garbage, Joseph's fictitious or real coat of many colors?, Noah's fictitious or real ark?, frantic pie-throwing, car-chasing, and stabbings without number. Replace all this entertainment with real life and real challenges—encouraging your children to make something of themselves. Reclaim those hours for high purposes; the more hours, the better. Achieving greatness begins the moment a child is born. Hours are investments in one sort of capital or another. You hold the keys.

What do you DO with a child?

From the day that each child is born, you begin to progressively and incrementally **grow him into an awesome adult**.

God grows the child, but you trim and prune and water and tweak the child. God is the seed giver, but you are the gardener. And make no mistake: the gardener has an enormous influence on outcomes. Take two gardeners: one is scattered, unfocused, preoccupied, and lazy. The other is focused, industrious, careful and attentive. Both are responsible for rose bushes. One garden is left to grow wild; the other is tamed into a world-famous rose garden. Roses bloom in both gardens, but those in the untended garden are covered over with thorns and weeds. God *always* does His part (the rose/child *will* grow up)—but what about *your* part? What sort of garden/rosebush will this child become? (Even though *all* the dynamics won't be within your hands—you can't control all of the effects of original DNA, convoluted circumstances, health issues, accidents and injuries, and counterproductive input from friends, neighbors and relatives—but you can greatly influence all the dynamics that *are* within your reach.)

Begin with the end in view. Where are you headed with your child? Are you and the children flopping around the living room, taken up with every novel idea that comes around and other people's agendas for your day, or do you have some strong plans of your own to implement with your children? Decide where you are headed. Protect those plans from outsiders' distractions and from your own lesser matters and endless errands.

This is how parenting works in every area of a child's life: if you intend for your child to someday live in a clean, **orderly** home as an adult, not in a pigsty, you begin by teaching your two-year-old how to empty the trash, using a tiny trashcan that is just his size. By the time he's a 10-year-old he ought to know how to vacuum and fix a meal or two by himself.

If you intend for your child to become articulate, have a large **vocabulary**, and charm people in any conversation, you begin by talking to your baby as if he were an adult, reading Isaac Watt's hymns aloud to him while you nurse. By the time he is 10, you're making sure he has read a good 500 wholesome books or so (and can talk about them to you): books that are full of real history—missionary biographies—how-to books.   Skimp over much of the fantasy/twaddle. Then increase it to a thousand more books. (At our website, download *Melanie Ellison's Favorite Books for Godly Children*—a list of over 100 best-of-the-best books for children.) Then borrow them for free through inter-library loan or buy them used and inexpensively from AbeBooks.com or BookFinder.com and specific sources suggested on that list).

If you don't want your child to be a sluggard as an adult, you progressively and incrementally put the bee on him to **work** when he is four.

If you want him to have a chance at becoming a good **musician**, have him listen to classical music every day while he is still in diapers, take him to symphony orchestra rehearsals, and gently tap out rhythms on his back. (Make sure he never gets near rock music; as sadly happens in countless families. Rock music is now conclusively known to become progressively addictive and can completely dive-bomb all of your best efforts at parenting.)

If you want him to be at ease eventually while **eating** international and gourmet dishes, you give him little amounts of a wide variety of foods and tastes when he is three years old. Set a small portion of these on his plate at each dinner and require him to eat them before having more of his favorite foods. Particularly introduce him to a wide variety of steamed vegetables, slathered with lemon and coconut oil. Incrementally develop his palette. Grow a healthy child by insisting upon healthy habits/choices from the get-go. Make junk food unavailable.

If you want him to **reverence** God, begin reading Scripture to your child when he is still in utero. (There is only a thin wall of skin between you.) When he's born, replace airhead nursery rhymes and twaddle with substance, and start reading to him from easy versions of Scripture. Teach him to know all the books of the Bible in order so he can flip to them easily. Conquer and review two or three book names a day. Teach the key people and the key events. Then progress to looking for the high voltage underneath specific verses, together. Start today with your six-month-old. Outline the cover with his little finger, while saying "This is God's love letter to *you*! Isn't that exciting that He wrote to *you*!"

Say a **Scripture verse** over your child every time you change his diapers. If you say the same verse all week, in a year he will know 52 verses by osmosis. Likewise, sing a hymn a week, and by the end of the year he will know 52 hymns. When you rise up and when you sit down, grow a spiritual child (Deuteronomy chapters 4-6). *If you only concentrate on academics or talents, or sports, you COULD raise a brilliant murderer!* **Life must have a WHY, not just a how.**

If you want him to know how to **manage money and make a living**, help him start his home based business when he is five years old. Teach him how to take advantage of any wholesome income stream whenever and wherever it is flowing. If the lady next door wants her chickens watched and she will pay him money, then drop everything and go do it, because tomorrow maybe no one wants their chickens watched. And then teach him how to make a few income streams of his own. Make something that is irresistible to others, such as brownies, or improved small gardening equipment. Every entrepreneur starts with baby steps. Producing brownies may eventually be replaced with producing computer microchips, or growing lettuce with sound waves.

Begin by paying him 10 cents to collect 10 rocks for your new garden rock walkway or to iron his sister's shirts. Teach him to be on the look-out to provide services to others in some better way. Hard-working immigrants do this. They raise their children in and around the work ethic, and thereby out-produce many who have lived in American ghettos for generations. Jews did this when they established the nation of Israel from scratch, and vaulted to the top of European exports—out of barren rocky ground. Begin to train your children in economics when they are one-year-old. "This is a nickel; this is a dime." Then a few years later, add the thought: "If you do this extra job, you'll hear this dime clink in your jar."

If you want him to be meticulously **honest** as an adult, strongly land on his first lie, and spin his head at the consequences of having told it.

If you want to grow a **winsome** adult, teach the child a hearty handshake, a broad smile, and the habit of looking in people's eyes while listening to them.

If you want to grow a very **capable, confident** adult, grow as many life skills as possible, incrementally and progressively, all through the years. These could include barbering, elk hunting, sewing alterations, car mechanics, speed-typing 90 wpm, bread-making, carpentry, piano accompaniment, and electricians' skills. Grow these, and many more, developing ever-deeper levels of competence. The more an individual knows how to do, the less dependent he is upon experts and the more helpful he becomes to others in nearly every situation or emergency, to say nothing of the money he'll save. To grow a broadly skilled child, deliberately take this ground inch by inch.

The gardener bends the tree and ties it to the fence, tilts the plant to get the most sun, protects it from tornadoes when young, sets it out IN the storms when it's older, hardens off the top, and strengthens the root. Parenting is a full-time job with no pay raises, but if you do it well, your future reward could well bowl you over with joy. Parent with everything you've got, because it is a 100-yard dash across time and then it is over. Parent *now* like there is no tomorrow.

A broader view of each child's future

Focus on life skills. What will your child need, the day after he gets married? Progressively help your child solve the **money** question and the **relational** question along with his

academics. Twelve years spent on all books and aimless activities isn't going to cut it. When he emerges from high school or college, real life will smack him in the face like a wet towel if you haven't prepared him in all three of these areas.

Does he know how a dollar is optimally earned, saved and invested for a lifetime of zero financial stress? Will he be able to hold his marriage together over rough patches and will he be able to hold his children's affections after they leave home, because of how he treated them before? In all of his social interchanges has he been trained to consistently bless people or does he consistently irritate all who know him? Does he know real history, English and math, well? Can he brandish them about and actually use them?

Did he emerge from school with a lifetime habit of continual reading and self-education? In short, does he always have a book with him? We live many more years beyond school than we spent in it, and if the lifetime habit of continual self-education has not been established, life will be limited and much will be missed.

Your biggest job is staying ahead of acquiring top-notch books for your child to read (even picking his recreational books). It is up to you to run ahead of him to get the books to dangle as the carrot of inspiration in front of him all through the years. The more quality books he can get under his belt, the higher his life will soar.

Teach your children that life has endless possibilities and that it leaves one breathless to fit it all in. By your own daily example give them a zest for living. Never allow the phrase

"I'm bored!" Stay ahead of them with activities. Remember once again, "Busy children are happy children."

Train your children to have a good work ethic, and garner an actual portfolio of written character references from all of these lesser jobs. The presentation of a résumé with comments like: "I not only liked the quality of his work but the SPIRIT with which he worked," will charm any future employer. There will be no end of otherwise closed doors in top-quality positions.

When you come to the time for career planning, look back over what your child *did* well—not merely what interested him. Think back: Which aspect of a project invariably grabbed his attention? The speaking aspect, or the mechanical? The sorting aspect or the marketing? etc. He must enjoy the *daily tasks* of his eventual career, not just be interested in the *overall idea*. A misfit lawyer became a clock maker in mid-life and it turned his frustrated life into one of daily joy.

Your child may be no judge of his actual aptitudes. When asked what she wants to be, your daughter may reply, "I want to be Miss America or an astronaut!" It takes your objectivity to identify and point out what their consistent childhood successes imply for their future.

He gently leads those who are with young.

And so we draw now to a close. This book was written to enlarge your vision for your own home. If you find yourself hovering somewhere between inspiration and feeling overwhelmed, remember that Rome wasn't built in a day. Keep in mind that these thoughts are the fruit of years and years of searching for the principles that make a mother wise and a home an "earlier heaven." Do not let your heart be discouraged. Let these principles inspire and encourage you, instead. If you simply veer north in each of the areas described here, you will experience more order, more joy and more meaning than you ever have before. Knowing where you are headed is half of the battle, even if you don't get there overnight! Remember, He is Lord of your today, as well as Lord of where you will be in the future.

Understanding *what* to do and *how* to do it is 95% of any new task. Any woman can have a renaissance of her "own-making" in her own home—all it takes is know-how.

INDEX

Contact us:

If you were helped by this book, and want to, drop us an email at info@homeschoolhowtos.com and tell us how. Visit us online at www.homeschoolinghowtos.com

Pass it on:

Also, consider telling a friend about this book. Give her the opportunity to have the helps you now have. If you do, no doubt, a number of happier children and pleasantly surprised husbands will thank you for it.

Made in the USA
San Bernardino, CA
10 June 2016